The Way of Compassion

...into the heart of the
Seven Sorrows of Mary

Father Richard C. Antall

D1319147

Our Sunday Visitor Publishing Division
Our Sunday Visitor, Inc.
Huntington, Indiana 46750

Our Sunday Visitor Publishing Division
Our Sunday Visitor, Inc.
200 Noll Plaza
Huntington, IN 46750

ISBN: 0-87973-854-5
LCCCN: 97-67057

Cover design by Rebecca Heaston
Illustrations by Robert F. McGovern

Printed in the United States of America

854

Table of Contents

To my mother, Theresa, who taught me to love
Our Mother

Introduction

■■■■■ ■ ■■■ ■ ■■ ■■ ■■ ■■ ■ ■■ ■ ■■■ ■ ■ ■

Why the Sorrows of Mary?

We should never give up on the conversion of anybody, least of all ourselves. When some of us think about how much we have changed over the years, it ought to make us feel optimistic for others. Grace works all kinds of reversals in our lives. God is not through with us while we live and breathe, and the thought is a consolation.

I think of my own case. When I was a seminarian, I had little use for the Rosary or any special devotions. I never denied their value as some of my brother seminarians did, questioning the Rosary or mocking its value, but I denied their value in practice because I never made time for them. Some pious devotions, I thought, are just too passé to be rescued. It turns out that I was the one who needed rescuing.

Once, as a recently ordained priest, I went to a shrine of the Sorrowful Mother. The seminary did not teach us about integrating our intellectual knowledge with piety, and, in fact, I think it had served to make some of us less pious than we were at the start of our formation. "No one is less reverent than the sacristan," says a refrain in Spanish, and that often applies in the case of the seminarian.

And so we were at a small chapel that had several quite terrible paintings of the Virgin Mary crying or looking like she was thinking about it. It was not art, but what is called kitsch — inferior art that makes a grab at the emotions and not the heart or the head.

"Now that," I joked to those with me, "is really a sorrowful mother." What I meant, of course, was that the painting itself was not a masterpiece. I spoke flippantly.

Today, my judgement of the picture would probably be more harsh than ever, but I doubt that I would joke about it — not because I have given up joking or have converted into a some kind of plaster saint, but because I have a new respect for all that is meant by the devotion to Mary as the Sorrowful Mother. I no longer see the devotion as maudlin or as an example of exaggerated sentimentalism.

I have had what one of my professors in the seminary calls an intellectual conversion, the understanding component of conversion. This means a conversion on the level of ideas — not the most important part of conversion, but necessary for those of us who perhaps have studied too much for our own good. I have come to understand that, at its core, the devotion to the Sorrowful Mother is a portrait in what it means to suffer with Jesus. One of my favorite books of theological reflection is Dietrich Bonhoeffer's *The Cost of Discipleship*. Bonhoeffer was a German Lutheran pastor who died in a concentration camp because of his involvement in resistance to Hitler. At a time when very few put their lives on the line to stand up for basic Christianity, Bonhoeffer gave a shining example of commitment.

His thoughts reflected the burning cauldron of his experience as a pastor in what he called the Confessing

Church. These were German Protestants who would not accept the status quo that Hitler and Nazism represented. One of his ideas was that too often church people present an idea of "cheap grace," a kind of no-strings-attached belief in Christianity as a comfortable way to live. Bonhoeffer would have agreed with Cardinal Newman, who had for his motto for much of his life the phrase "Holiness before peace."

Mary the Sorrowful Mother is really another portrait in the courage necessary to follow Jesus. The cost of discipleship in her life is what the famous Seven Sorrows try to map out for us. She was the woman of faith beset by trials all her life, but her heart was true as fire-tried gold. If we want to find an example of endurance, of loyalty, of a readiness to serve God in whatever way that might be, of a communion with the life and sacrifice of Christ, we need look no further. The Seven Sorrows are a symbolic language of discipleship. The images, like the mysteries of the Rosary, communicate much more than some doctrinal statements. They beg an identification in Mary's journey of faith and a similar response to Jesus, the Crucified One.

The devotion can speak to us perhaps more than words. The emblem of a heart pierced with a sword for the love of Jesus could be the new Christian badge of courage. The older I get the more I see how close all of us live to the edge of sadness. What can all this suffering mean? How is the human heart to find a way to exist in this broken world without becoming hard?

"It is a world of disappointment," wrote Dickens in Oliver Twist, "often to those hopes that do our nature its highest honor." Where can we seek comfort that is not escape, strength that will be turned against no one, courage that will allow us to be free of our own pettiness?

There is a Joni Mitchell song that was popular when I was growing up which says,

> "Don't it always seem to go
> That you don't know what you've got
> 'til it's gone?"

This could be the song of the Church in recent times. We have lost a lot even as we have gained a great deal in the years since Vatican II.

I think that some time will have to pass before we understand how to properly integrate the Council in our faith life. Since I have had the great fortune to work in Latin America, I can see that, in many respects, the American model of applying the Council is characteristic of our lifestyles and habits. Americans have a fascination with the new. It is the subject of parody how some products, like detergent soaps, are not just "new" but "all new." If a product is really "all new," what relationship does it have with the name modified by the adjective "new"? Some people see life more in terms of discontinuity than continuity. Jesus spoke to this issue when he used the example of the steward who knew how to bring from the storehouse both the new and the old (Mt 13:52). The Latin mentality is more "both/and" than "either/or."

However, our way is not the only way. Other places and other people do not look at the difference between before and after the Council as though it were as dramatic a change as between the Old and New Testaments. Many people conserved the old devotions even as they renewed along the lines of the Council, with greater lay leadership and more Scripture. I think it is an American handicap to think that renewed means totally new. That sometimes goes against ordinary psychology. Think, for instance, about what sacred space means to most people. Why were people so upset with the new theater-churches in which Cromwell's troops would have been proud to worship? Many post-Conciliar intellectuals went overboard — not in interpreting the texts of Vatican II, which were well-integrated in the Tradition, but in interpreting the "spirit," an area in which there was much more room for ambiguity.

Sometimes you have to miss something in order to appreciate it. This idea helps explain to me some of the movements in the Church in America today. There is an explosion of popular piety — Eucharistic and Marian. There are some concerns about these things, of course, but what is illustrated by people who are fascinated with the supernatural is that there is some kind of gap in their religious experience. The religious imagination needs more than whitewashed-worship areas, *Reader's Digest* humanism, or group dynamics. It demands a vision of eternity, a backdrop of heaven and hell. It has need of angels and saints and the experience of grace in the details of life. It requires the concrete imagery of popular devotion.

Obviously, there are styles of expression in culture. There are certain characteristics of an epoch and a culture. The Church has always provided a religious vocabulary to identify the inarticulate longings of the human spirit. This vocabulary is based not on concepts or abstractions, but on real people and relationships. Not holiness in essence, but holiness as it is expressed in the lives of the saints; not patient endurance taken abstractly, but in the suffering of the one who was the Mother of the Savior.

Classic Catholicism is what C.S. Lewis called a "thick" religion. I think of it as parallel to "deep dish" pizza. You can get a thin crust or you can get a thick-crust pizza pie with all kinds of ingredients. Too much of what was called Vatican II Catholicism was a thin-crust approach, leaving out some of the elements that most appeal to and nourish the human heart. As a result, or at least concomitant with this paler version of Tradition, people have been obsessed with old heresies and new, from spiritualism to New Age. What is the meaning of this angelology which practically neglects to speak about God and Jesus, or the longing for transcendence expressed in belief in extraterrestrial life? If religion becomes an unimaginative thin gruel, some will throw other things into the pot.

One of the perennial crises of the Church is to find ways to help people associate their lives with the life of Jesus Christ. Today, there is competition for the transcendent imagination of humanity. If the Church cannot give people a sense of the mystical, some will go to Eastern religions. Others will make religions out of whatever strikes their fancy. There is much lamenting about fundamentalist churches and militant Islam, but there is no appreciation of what appeals in a movement self-confident in its imagination of the transcendent. Hunger for transcendence is the basic religious instinct, not desire to know the latest intellectual fashion.

Religious imagery is a vocabulary of transcendence. Catholicism has always been noted for its ability to communicate the there and beyond in the right here and now.

Our Tradition has done so by focusing on the Incarnate God, an Incarnate God who was fully human, with the usual range of human constellations and experiences, although not of personal sin.

So the Christ has a mother. A great prophet is his cousin. He calls disciples and some of them are brothers, and their mother is somehow asked to get involved. One of his closest followers ends up betraying him. The Catholic tendency to draw out the details of the Incarnation in their human applications is present right in the New Testament. How else to explain why the baby in the womb of Elizabeth leaps with joy? Why else would an older kinswoman say to a younger, "Who am I that the mother of my Lord should come to me?"

In every age, the renewal of the Church has depended on the religious imagination of common people. By themselves, intellectuals have never been able to renew the Church. After every doctrinal crisis, the saints were the ones to achieve the reform of the Church. The intellectuals might identify the problems with heresy, but it took a hero like Athanasius, allied to the desert monks who were the opposite of intellectuals, to defeat Arianism. In the Middle Ages, it was not the debating skills of the scholars but the love of Francis of Assisi and Clare that renewed the Church. St. Teresa of Ávila, St. Ignatius of Loyola, even St. Charles Borromeo and St. Francis Borgia were able to give strength to the Catholic Reformation in a time of religious chaos because they appealed to religious imagination.

The renewal of the Church in our age will be popular, also. This will stun the intellectuals even though this is the oldest dynamic in our Tradition. St. Paul talked about how God had scorned "the wisdom of the wise," and Jesus himself marveled how his Father had revealed his truth to the "merest children."

An important part of that popular revival will be to rescue some of the treasure of Tradition. Jesus spoke about the wise steward who brought forth both the new and old from his storehouse. For some time, Catholics have been looking only for the new. Certain fads should have had the "not to be sold after" or "use by" dates like perishable items from the grocery because they were not made to last. Even some in the Church figured that Bible translations should be changed continuously like almanacs.

An English writer once said that ideas have a generational dynamic. Young men, he said, are sometimes more inclined to take their grandfather's side than that of their father. I wonder if we don't have a little of that in terms of religion. For a while, everything stressed discontinuity. What if we need to see how continuity and integration are the hallmarks of Catholicism, and some of the leadership missed the train? What if we need a little more of that old-time religion with its deep-dish approach? There are times and seasons for everything. Maybe the pendulum has to swing back a bit.

A relative of mine, born Lutheran but now a practicing Presbyterian, once told me that her minister said he thought that when the Protestant founding fathers reformed the Church, they reformed a little too much. He found much that was appealing in Catholic iconography and religious Tradition. I think that many mainline churches find themselves in a similar position.

A Lutheran church in town regularly borrows cassocks for its celebration of Tenebrae in Holy Week. Catholic churches are unwisely (and illicitly) throwing out kneelers while Protestant congregations are putting them in. Does it have to be gone before we know what we've got? Obviously, I think not. That is why I have written this book. It was inspired by my experience in Latin America on several levels. First, I found a Church there which combined a devotional life built on traditional elements with the Conciliar renewal. A church of martyrs for social justice was also the church of the Rosary and the Stations of the Cross. A picture of murdered priests or nuns found a spot on the wall next to an altar adorned with old saints. Continuity was stressed, not rupture. In fact, the traditional devotions, especially those dealing with the suffering of Christ, were good vehicles for understanding what was happening in present persecutions.

On other levels, the experience of the Church in Latin America was very challenging. I read a book by a missionary once who described his experience of Catholicism in the context of a non-Christian culture as a "reinventing" of Christianity. For me, my mission years in El Salvador were a rediscovery of Catholicism. The same religion that fired my imagination in childhood allowed these poor people to find consolation in suffering and transcendent power to convert themselves first of all, and then to announce the kingdom of Christ to others.

Naturally, I experienced the prayer and the life of the people as one. The people in cultures other than our own often do not departmentalize the sacred the way we modern North Americans do. Religion in our culture is one aspect of life, but it is still only one, even if we give it some kind of honorary first place. For the poor people I worked with, religion was not one category — it was everything. God was not restricted to acting within certain predefined limits; he was the backdrop of all existence. I saw people in the big old churches, evidently pouring their hearts out before prayer-prompters like crucifixes and statues. Prayer is often felt with a great intensity.

I remember traveling to Guatemala and visiting the cathedral in the capital city. I have to confess that, sometimes, I visited the old churches more to look around at the colonial art than to pray. It is hard not to be a tourist in places with so much history. But I got a glimpse of something interesting that trip. In the cathedral, I saw a North American friend kneeling at the side altar on which there was an image of *"La Dolorosa,"* the name in Spanish for the Sorrowful Mother. The statue was very traditional, dressed in flowing robes, with tear-painted cheeks and a great sword through the heart on the outside of the figure. Piety is seldom expressed among brother priests. We are usually careful to draw the curtain on our own life of prayer. But there was this young priest, whose ideas were sometimes much too modern for me, praying like a campesino and talking to the Virgin Mother like a lost child. It was, to say the least, an unexpected grace.

But also, I understood the reaction in a moment. When you see what 1 would call the practical, contemplative aspect of the faith of these people, it enables you to do things you might not do at home. My heart wanted me to kneel and pray also. I was suddenly no longer a tourist but a Catholic responding to an artistic vision of Our Mother, the woman of suffering.

Of course there was also something else there that helped the prayer inspired by Our Lady of Sorrows. Some of the women praying in the cathedral were symbols of suffering in their own way. One does not need to know them individually to understand that their faith is their consolation in the face of poverty, disappointment, injustice, and the lack of love in their lives. Such women see in "*La Dolorosa*" a kind of idealized image of themselves. This beautiful lady has also known sorrow, the kind that cuts your heart in two.

The best consolers are those who have been through pain and suffering themselves. In the case of prayer to Mary the Sorrowful One, I think that the dynamic goes even further. It is a question of mutual consolation. The feeling of sympathy for the saints and the suffering Christ which is what I regard as classic Catholicism is still alive in Latin Christianity. Why not feel sorry for Mary? What can console and humanize like tenderness felt for others who also suffer?

I used to take Communion to an old lady from the south of France who had somehow found her way to Cleveland. She insisted that I talk to her in my feeble French, and she cooked me wonderful meals when I visited her. Because I had a French translation of the Bible, I would read a little for her in my awful accent. Once I read a bit about Jesus' passion — it must have been around Holy Week — and she said something that sounded very funny to me.

"*Pauvre Jesus,*" she sighed. "*Si jeune.*" "Poor Jesus, he was such a young man." I thought her sympathy a bit misplaced at first. Who was she to regret the short life of Jesus? Did she really get the whole story? I wondered. Now,

I take a different view. Anything we can show in the way of compassion is something precious. Our meditation on the suffering of Jesus should include the feeling of the injustice of all that was done to him, even that he should be struck down in what we regard as the prime of life.

Many times I think that one of our typical problems in the U.S. is that we don't want to take suffering seriously. We cannot see it as inevitable; we are always trying to diminish it. You can see that even in some images of Jesus in our churches and institutions. Father Benedict Groeschel, the Capuchin preacher, has rightly criticized the "trampoline Jesus" of bourgeois Catholicism. When the image of Jesus on the cross appears more like a gymnast than a man tortured to his death, says the friar, something is wrong.

The Sorrows of Mary are a counterpart to meditating on the Stations of the Cross or the Sorrowful Mysteries of the Rosary. Mary, as always, the stand-in for all disciples, had a particularly challenging life. Popular piety could see that Jesus' mother had to suffer very much, too. The Seven Sorrows are moments in Mary's cost of discipleship. They enable us to meditate on the passion of Jesus as it is reflected in the sufferings of others.

For me, the Sorrows "work" because they enable me to do two things. The first is to build up my sense of relationship with Mary. Christ gave her to us as a mother when he hung upon the cross. Imagining her life is helpful to me because it makes me understand better how she models patience and sacrifice. Second, this devotion helps me to make sense or at least to see meaning in some of the suffering I have witnessed, especially among the poor.

This book is about Mary and it is about the suffering

of some women whom I have known and admired. I have wept with some of them, prayed for all of them, and I have taken to heart their pain. I see in their experience icons of the Sorrows of Mary.

The Sorrows, which I confess to having only recently learned, are as follows: (1) the prophecy of St. Simeon at the Presentation in the Temple; (2) the Flight into Egypt; (3) the child Jesus lost and then found in the Temple; (4) the sight of Jesus carrying the cross; (5) his crucifixion; (6) the piercing of his heart with the soldier's lance and the descent from the cross; and (7) the burial of Jesus.

What I intend to do in this little book is reflect on each of the Sorrows, comparing the experience of Mary with the suffering of some contemporary women. I met these women because of my serving in the mission, and I know Mary better for having known them and their stories.

Preamble

The Number Seven

Why *Seven* Sorrows of Mary? Surely we are not taking this as a literal accounting, as if she experienced only seven discrete moments of sorrow in the course of her life. The number is, rather, convenient and symbolic.

Seven is a number with great psychic resonance. Most people would say without thinking that the number seven is lucky. It is a superstition that is usually harmless, but reflects nevertheless that our faithless age is not an age of reason. Magic still appeals to people, whether it is astrology or the strategies some use to think of lottery numbers. Perhaps it is all because our hearts are restless and eagerly — but not wisely — seek for what is beyond us.

The number seven seems to have a certain importance even in the Bible. Creation is realized in seven days, a pattern in time that still holds in the world. The French revolutionaries once tried to change the week to a period of ten days and met with fierce resistance. The seven-day period is part of the rhythm of world religions, government, business, and news.

Other Biblical references to seven abound. Read the Lord's battle instructions for Joshua at the siege of Jericho in Joshua, chapter six, verses two through four:

> "I have delivered Jericho and its king into your power. Have all the soldiers circle the city, marching once around it. Do this for six days, with seven priests carrying ram's horns ahead of the ark. On the seventh day march around the city seven times, and have the priests blow the horns."

Isaiah mentions the seven gifts of the Holy Spirit, something which has become a pattern of Christian piety and the liturgy of confirmation. In the New Testament, not only are the gifts repeated, but several instances of seven are obvious. After the second miracle of the multiplication of the loaves and fishes, there were seven baskets of food left over. The book of the Acts describes the early Church and gives special emphasis to the seven deacons named to meet the material obligations of Christian ministry.

The Apocalypse, which is a great code of biblical cross-references, has the seven seals and the negative proof of the specialness of the number seven in the unholiness of 666. The truth is that the number seven, if not lucky in the superstitious sense, is at least symbolic of something more than counting. It represents a kind of perfection of justice, something hinted at in the advice to forgive your brother seventy times seven (Mt 18:22).

The perfection of seven relates also to the number of

the sacraments of Christ's Church. The seven sacraments are seven deacons serving us, and we receive from those seven baskets filled by the miracle of Jesus' power. The Catholic, who knows God is always close to us, is especially sensitive to His presence through the seven sacraments. They are not only seven doors to the sacred; they are also encounters with God. They are not only divine interventions in our life, but also sources of ongoing communion.

Grace in our lives can take a sevenfold manifestation. When I was in the seminary, a widower was studying for the sacrament of orders. We used to tease him that all his efforts were so that he could say that he had received every sacrament. That is not a likely scenario for the average Christian, but we can all appreciate that the sacraments are of and for the Church and thus include us all in some way or another. Surely I need not receive the sacrament of matrimony to appreciate its importance. The fact that I cannot receive it should, if anything, make me see its ecclesial dimension better.

The sevenfold nature of grace revealed in the sacraments can help us see the congruence of the Seven Sorrows of Mary. The devotion is a meditation on the sadness that was an inescapable part of the vocation of the Mother of God. The mystical association of seven helps one understand the transcendent meaning attached to the suffering of the Mother of God. The Seven Sorrows are coordinates on a map of the life of Mary. They are seven chapters for her biography which constitutes a special path to follow Jesus, Mary's way of compassion.

There are styles in piety as inevitable as styles in clothing and manners. There are those who find some old things interesting and others who find them merely difficult. Devotions are much involved with style. We cannot adopt old styles like someone going to a costume ball. There is always need for adaptation. Some of the old styles of piety were mere sentimentalism. We should never be satisfied with what is merely superficial, as sentimentalism is. I do not advocate some kind of return to the schmaltzy here. Maybe they weren't so schmaltzy in their day, but some devotions need to be adapted according to modern styles and manners. This means giving to the heart of their message a new form of expression. This is especially important in terms of relating our prayer life and our living.

The basic human truth that was the foundation of so many devotions is what is beyond certain vocabularies and styles. This basic human truth, as Cardinal Newman said, is that "The heart is commonly reached, not through the reason, but through the imagination. Persons influence us, voices melt us, looks subdue us, deeds inflame us."

The images of devotion were successful sacramentals because of their resemblance to the religious imagination, something that is deep inside of us. "Heart speaks to heart," was another of Cardinal Newman's favorite sayings, and is precisely to the point here. The heart of the Sorrowful Mother speaks to our heart, and often tears are used instead of just words. I think it would be a loss of a good help to popular meditation on discipleship if we lost the devotion to the sufferings of the Mother of God. The model is at once humanly very accessible and attractive.

The Seven Sorrows of Mary are about a real, historical person. She was a woman who suffered a great deal. This is the truth so many of the poor and simple have understood in praying to Mary as the Mother of Sorrows. Imagination leads to sympathy, a word that is sometimes misinterpreted but which comes from the roots "to suffer with." When we can feel for other people, we actually suffer with them. That is why love is so difficult at times. The Seven Sorrows of Mary are about love and about a holy sympathy.

As her Son was a Man of Sorrows, so was she a woman of tremendous sorrows. In her we can see reflected the suffering of every mother, indeed of every man and woman who has believed in Christ and has suffered. This insight not only leads to the communion that is sympathy, but also frees us from ourselves.

The Seven Sorrows of Mary teach us about her suffering, but also about our suffering. We cry with Mary. An old Irish prayer has Mary invite us to "keen with" her, which means to enter into her sadness and even to cry out with her in an expression beyond words.

Seven Sorrows. A desperate kind of perfection in suffering, a plenitude of pain to go with the fullness of grace that Mary lived and was. A sorrow for every day of the week. A sorrow deep and incomparable, a fate that was not star-crossed, but which involved the cross like none other but One.

The most Blessed Virgin Mary has been called the Queen of Martyrs. Her life was a witness of the love that sacrifices us. St. Anselm said that there was a relentlessness about her grief that made it miraculous that Mary bore up under the pressure of it.

I can imagine some saying to themselves, "But what about the joy of the Resurrection? What about the happiness that communion with God's grace meant for Mary? Were not her consolations even greater than her sorrows?"

Clearly, that is true. But there are two important

questions at stake here. First, the glory of grace needs to be set off by a realistic look at the difficulty of life. Second, we tend to try to avoid plumbing the depths of God's mercy. The Sorrows of Mary are about the whole nine yards, as a common sports metaphor puts it. We cannot deny sorrow and pretend that we are praising God by doing so.

When I was a young priest ordained for just over a month, I lost my father. He had been sick for only four months, but had declined so rapidly that he hadn't been able to attend my first Mass. The experience of grace so fresh in my life, I naturally had a special sensitivity about death. I often found myself crying at funerals, even when I didn't know the deceased. My own grief gave me a key to the grief of others.

One day a woman talked to me about grief. Quoting with approval a priest that was a shirttail sort of relative to her, she said that crying at a funeral could be taken as a sign of doubt about the resurrection. The priest in question had not cried at his mother's funeral because he was convinced that she was in God's hands.

I felt the woman's words as a sort of reproach until I remembered about Jesus weeping at the grave of Lazarus. Our Lord entered completely into the experience of loss, even though he was about to raise Lazarus back to life. No one would argue that Jesus' tears were a sign of despair. Rather, they were emblems of his humanity, some of the most precious tears in human history because they say more about God's mercy that words could ever express.

There are so many things about Jesus that seem impossible for us to realize in our own life. We have so little real understanding. We have such conflicts within us. But one thing we can hope to imitate is the love of Jesus. It is nothing technical or abstract; it starts in the core of our personhood that we call the heart. We can imitate the tears of Jesus. We can sense the sadness of the most noble of hearts.

When I worked in El Salvador, some young people and the Franciscan Sisters from our school used to do the Stations of the Cross "*en vivo*" (acted out) on Good Friday. A young man would carry a cross and eventually be hung from it (we used ropes to tie him to the cross) on the steps of the Church. The "production" was quite dramatic, but also had a great deal of devotion attached to it. Some people would be in tears at the end.

Acting out the scenes of the meditation meant thinking about a thousand details. So and so was to stand here, the soldier would be there — all the stuff that theater demands and is called "blocking." Then we had to teach a little method acting. The actor had to feel the role to get it right. We were very fortunate in that regard, but all the work that was involved would make me crazy in the middle of Holy Week. I never got through the rehearsals without blowing up about the carelessness of some members of the cast, or their lack of discipline as we practiced in the streets of the town.

It was all worth it. I had never entered into the experience of the Stations before with such attention. For instance, we had to think about how to communicate Mary's participation with the cross of Jesus in the brief and silent encounter of the Fourth Station. The girl that played Mary usually cut onions and put them in a handkerchief so that she could have a stimulus to produce tears. One year, a girl put Vicks VapoRub under her eyes and was crying even after the whole thing was over.

Another girl told me that no other stimuli had been necessary. Emotion had welled up within her and she had "felt" the Station. The look exchanged by two amateur actors pretending, for the whole town, to be Mary and Jesus, was like a study in popular understanding of the crucifixion. The mother's pain, the look of a son who wanted to comfort his mother who suffered for him, were played out in an obvious but sincere way.

Meditation on the Seven Sorrows requires only that kind of sincerity. We put our hearts where our faith is. Even our emotions, as sloppy and tricky as they sometimes are, can be consecrated to grace. Shakespeare, in one of the greatest pieces of rhetoric ever written, the funeral oration of Marc Antony from the play "Julius Caesar," wrote the famous line, "If you have tears, prepare to shed them now." My intention is not to manipulate feelings in offering you these reflections about our common mother. But if there be tears, internal or otherwise, we should not be ashamed of them. Tears that spring from the contemplation of grace are neither foolish nor idle. Like holy water, we can use such tears to cleanse and sanctify us.

There is a devotion that comes from that treasure house of devotion which is Mexican piety, which is called a *pésame* to the Virgin. *Pésame* is the word in Spanish for condolences. It comes from the joining of the word "it is heavy to me." *Sentido pésame* is what people offer at wakes — "sincere condolences," which means pure co-suffering (Latin: *sincerus cum dolere*). The *pésame* of the Virgin is a prayer which expresses sympathy for each of Our Lady's sorrows. These sketches are intended to help us to take seriously each aspect of the sadness of the Virgin's life. They are a personal sort of *pésame* offered to the Virgin.

God grant us hearts that feel and love.

THE FIRST SORROW

The Sword of Prophecy

The woman came to tell me about some troubles in her marriage. She had reached a point where she had to talk to someone about her suffering just to maintain some sort of control of her emotions.

Isabel's story was a very sad one. Because her troubles were so great, she was thinking of her whole life as a single suffering. She not only wanted to tell me about the special circumstances of her present problem; she also wanted to tell me the whole story, how life had treated her from the beginning.

That beginning had for a symbol a bus trip she took with her mother when she was only ten years old. They left their home in the eastern part of the country to go to the capital. Even today, the roads are rough and buses are not like Greyhound's. Riding across the country means cramming into a school-bus-type vehicle and bouncing along dusty roads for six or seven hours. The heat is terrible, the crowding tremendous — even if people are not carrying their chickens and other paraphernalia — and the monotony is interrupted only by the crying of babies. The whole thing is an endurance test.

Isabel had never been on the trip and she did not really know how to get to her final destination. The bus trip, however, was not the principal challenge. She had to take care of her mother.

It would have been different, perhaps, if her mother had an illness that would have counted with the sympathy of the other passengers. The problem was that she was much too healthy. She flirted with most of the men on the bus and in the little towns where it stopped. It seemed that she never stopped talking and singing — at times to her daughter, sometimes to the strangers who traveled with them, but really essentially to herself. It was a dramatic monologue that ranged from laughing hysterically to crying hopelessly.

Isabel's mother had become a *loca,* a madwoman, and people were not reluctant to call her that, even in front of her young daughter. The young girl was taking her mother across the country to the nation's only psychiatric institution. Isabel was doing this because the only other person from the family who could help was her mother's sister, and she was caring for Isabel's younger brother, who was only six years old. Her own children and home situation supposedly prevented the aunt from doing more.

There was no one else to take this woman to the hospital. Isabel's father was gone, and that was good. His violence with her mother was the reason for the woman's illness. Of course Isabel had witnessed the terrible beatings her father had given her mother. She just hadn't the luxury of a breakdown to get those images from her tender memory.

At the hospital, the doctor gave the mother the usual sedatives and talked to the little girl who was the woman's caregiver.

"Your mother must take her pills every day," he told her, "And you must bring her back here every month on the date stamped on this card."

The child of ten took her mother home after the visit with the doctor. For the rest of her mother's life, Isabel had to worry about her. She could share the responsibility with no one. The little brother, who could never understand what was going on, grew to be a man and eventually developed drinking problems. The family's mental instability was revealed again in his violence and trouble with the law.

Once Isabel had to have her brother put in jail because he had brandished a knife at her husband. Her mother was also in the house and had immediately started a campaign to have the brother released. Their family life was an exaggerated kind of tragicomedy, with terrible scenes that were the scandal of the little town where we lived.

But that was later, much later, in the story. What interests me here is the thought of a young girl all alone in a terrible situation. To whom could she turn? On what could she rely? With which schoolmate could she discuss her problems with her mother? Whose life could be compared to hers?

For days her mother would be normal, then she would begin imagining things. Sometimes these would be harmless and even whimsical. Her mother could sew well and made artificial flowers. She always had a kind of sensitivity to colors and beauty and an undeniable creativity. But that creativity was also at the service of the darker side of her nature. The trauma with the father of her children expressed itself in her fascination with strangers, especially her fascination with weddings.

Many more times than once, Isabel had to take her mother out of churches because she would interrupt weddings claiming to be the woman the bridegroom had left behind. Her fate had become generalized in her own mind. Every bridegroom was the man who had left her, the beautiful bride the symbol of all she was cheated of.

When I talked to Isabel, I felt that I was seeing the struggles of a young girl trying to understand what was far beyond what most adults could hope to comprehend. The image of the bus trip was still so keen after more than twenty-five years. Her mother's sickness and the terrible struggles of her life were represented by that trip to the capital. She naturally associated it with the worst of the trials and tribulations of her life.

Isabel's first man didn't work out for her, perhaps because she always had to take care of her mother, perhaps because he was a man in the image of her father, and men were supposed to make you suffer. It was lucky for her that she had not married him, even though he had fathered her first child. She had too many responsibilities to support that kind of a man.

It is hard to describe my emotions on hearing her story. Sometimes priestly ministry is so intense. People tell you the story of broken lives and sufferings that cannot even be imagined. The sensitivity of the priest is both his strength and his weakness. Without some vulnerability, you cannot really listen to so much suffering without rebelling. With that vulnerability, and without taking advantage of spiritual resources, a man can get into trouble. The priest needs to relate everything back to his first commitment. He has to see Christ in all the brokenness he witnesses, and do so without being scandalized by the Incarnation of God in the midst of such sadness and imperfection.

Isabel's story moved me to tears, and has stayed with me through the years. It was present to me when we buried her mother and I saw the strain in the daughter's face. I feared for her sanity, too. Thank God, she pulled through.

Now that I am far away from the country where the drama of her life unfolded, I think of how Isabel's strange vocation compares to that of Our Lady of Sorrows.

The old Latin breviary for September 15, the Feast of the Seven Sorrows, has some readings taken from the Old Testament Book of Lamentations.

> What can I say for you,
> O daughter Jerusalem?
> What can I liken to you, that I
> may comfort you
> O virgin daughter of Zion?
> For vast as the sea is your
> ruin . . . (RSV 2:13).

The last image has special force for me because for seven and a half years I lived two blocks from the Pacific Ocean in my beloved El Salvador. Sometimes I would walk near the beach in the evening, and I remember with gratitude the beauty of the a starry night over the immensity of dark water. The ocean at night really gives an impression of infinity. To say that a disaster is as great as the sea is to say a great deal.

Now, I realize that I am going against what the reading says by holding up the example of Isabel and thus, of course, comparing her to the incomparable Virgin Mary. My only excuse is that even the idea of incomparability is based on at least a partial comparison. We have to have some parameters, some measuring sticks, even when looking at what is totally unique. All the examples I use in this book are really just to give some perspective, and reveal how I was able to understand the Sorrows of the Virgin better, in terms of other women.

When I try to imagine how a little girl like Isabel would feel in the strange new world of her mother's illness, I feel a terrible loneliness. I think that Mary's vocation of suffering must have been lonely too, so lonely that it would be comparable to the infinity of the sea. Lonely because, who could have understood it?

The Scripture scholars indicate that Mary was probably a very young woman at the time of the Annunciation. The marriageable age was thirteen or fourteen. At the most, the Blessed Mother was an adolescent when she undertook the extraordinary mission to serve God by being the mother of the Savior.

What a lonely young lady she had to be. St. Joseph was a good man, but evidently did not understand at first, because if he had, there would have been no need of the angel's revelation to him in his dreams. In fact, his goodness reveals the precariousness of the Virgin's life. His discretion was revealed in his decision to divorce Mary quietly, thus saving her life. What shows the goodness of one man illustrates the scariness of being a woman in such a time. A woman whose virtue was compromised faced the threat of capital punishment. The Virgin's vocation assumed that risk, even though her virtue was the mirror of all virtue.

But even that challenge is not the First Sorrow, nor the journey to Bethlehem, which has received so much attention in homilies and pious reflection. The First Sorrow is called the Sword of Prophecy because that is what Simeon predicted for Mary. The sword that pierced her heart is the emblem of her tragic vocation of suffering. It includes all the sorrows within itself by virtue of symbol. The Sword of the Prophecy was symbolic of a destiny of suffering, cutting to the heart of the Virgin's existence.

We should review the circumstances of the prophecy, which is recounted in Luke 2:22-35:

> When the days were completed for their purification according to the law of Moses, they took him up to Jerusalem to present him to the Lord, just as it is written in the law of the Lord, "Every male that opens the womb shall be consecrated to the Lord," and to offer the sacrifice of "a pair of turtledoves or two young pigeons," in accordance with the dictate in the law of the Lord.
>
> Now there was a man in Jerusalem whose name was Simeon. This man was righteous and devout, awaiting the con-

solation of Israel, and the Holy Spirit was upon him. It had been revealed to him by the holy Spirit that he should not see death before he had seen the Messiah of the Lord. He came in the Spirit into the temple; and when the parents brought in the child Jesus to perform the custom of the law in regard to him, he took him into his arms and blessed God, saying:

"Now, Master, you may let
  your servant go
in peace, according to your
  word,
  for my eyes have seen your
  salvation,
which you prepare in sight of all
  the peoples,
a light for revelation to the
  Gentiles,
and glory for your people
  Israel."

The child's father and mother were amazed at what was said about him; and Simeon blessed them and said to Mary his mother, "Behold, this child is destined for the fall and rise of many in Israel, and to be a sign that will be contradicted (and you yourself a sword will pierce) so that the thoughts of many hearts may be revealed."

There are a number of key phrases in the passage that merit some comment. Scholars have wondered why, in the first verse quoted, St. Luke says "their" purification. Obviously, the law required only the purification of the mother. It was a taboo for a woman to enter the temple either during her menstruation or before forty days from the birth of a son (eighty after the birth of a daughter).

The Book of Leviticus has some detail on this ritual in the twelfth and the fifteenth chapters. The mysterious power of the cycle of reproduction caused a certain awe among the ancient Hebrews. Their expression of that awe is alien to us. We can hardly understand their ideas of cultic impurity because such notions are not part of the New Testament; in fact, they are eliminated by Christ's command. It was indicative of a certain type of respect for the sacred and the powers of nature, we can say, and little else.

As a priest in the missions, I sometimes heard confessions by women who were concerned about old Testament prohibitions, but I always was able to reassure them that such laws no longer were applicable. However, I should mention that there was a custom in the United States of "churching" a woman forty days after childbirth, which consisted in little more than a special blessing given at the side altar. Perhaps this was a holdover from Leviticus, or a kind of remembrance of the Purification of the Virgin Mary, but it recalls another interesting fact: in the days before the Second Vatican Council, the mother would often not be present for the baptism of her children. This, of course, made for a more important role for the godmother in the ceremony and in the folklore of the sacrament.

Why then, "their" purification if only Mary was expected to complete a certain time period away from the temple and all the formally sacred? Some say that St. Luke is making one thing the offering for Jesus with the purification of Mary. Others say that it was the slip of the pen, perhaps reflecting that the concept of ritual impurity was foreign already to Luke and so he lumped together two ideas. I wonder if such a slip might not be taken as a kind of solidarity between mother and child, a solidarity of experience that was always close to an identity in intimacy. The togetherness of their experience is, after all, one of the underlying premises of these reflections.

Really, the law demanded two different sacrifices, one that had to do with childbirth and every mother, and another that applied to just the firstborn child. Every firstborn creature was considered to belong to God and therefore had to be "redeemed" in the sense that something had to be given to God instead. This was explained by Exodus 13:14 as having a reference to the last plague of Egypt, when God caused the angel of death to sweep through the land, bringing about the death of the firstborn of all but the families who had celebrated Passover and were protected by the blood of the lamb.

St. Luke does not specify the two sacrifices, but he

obviously has an interest in a detail of the sacrifice. He records that it was the sacrifice demanded of the poor that Mary presented. It is a small kind of detail, but it speaks to us a great deal. The family of Jesus qualified as the poor. To use rough equivalents, Mary and Joseph would have more to do with families that qualify for food stamps than with the middle class. The poverty of Jesus was a basic datum of his experience, even from his first days. Thus it was for Mary and Joseph. How much more that should make us think of the poor!

Now to the actual words that express the first sorrow, "And a sword shall pierce your heart." It is a sign of the reverence for the memory of Mary in the life of the Church that this reference was never taken literally. Because the life of Mary was part of the memory of the Church, no one ever argued that Mary was executed by the sword. Rather, a symbolic interpretation was given to the prophecy of St. Simeon, something one translation of the Bible I consulted underscores by leaving out the sword and saying only, "and you, too, will be pierced to the heart."

Some effort of imagination is in order for us here. We all know that a mother hopes for the best for her child. Part of the sadness we feel about babies born with serious problems is the fact that the parents must worry from the start of life about the consequences of defects or other diseases.

How was it for Mary that day? She was hearing that every step her child would take, every milestone in his life, would lead him inevitably to an adulthood full of conflict and rejection. Now rejection in terms of the standing or falling of "many in Israel" would have to be a dangerous proposition. Jesus was forty days old, and St. Simeon was predicting his crucifixion. St. Bernard of Clairvaux said that the Passion of our Lord began as soon as he was born. Mary's consciousness of that Passion, that slow grinding of the wheels of fate that would take Jesus to Calvary, has to be dated from the day of her purification in the temple.

Tell a mother that her son will end up being executed and that prophecy will color all her perceptions about the childhood and youth of the child. Even joys will seem partial, because of what waits. The icon of Our Lady of Perpetual Help has Mary consoling the infant Jesus, who is looking at the instruments of torture the angels are showing him. Medieval religious art played with the same theme in any number of paintings of the childhood of Christ. The boy Jesus would prick his finger on a thorn and his mother would contemplate him with fear and sadness in her eyes.

When we see an evil coming, it is all the more unbearable. And that is what the Sword of Prophecy represented for Mary. The Irish mother in John M. Synge's "Riders to the Sea" reflects the fatality of living close to something that threatens the well-being of her family and the life of her men. That pressure of fatality was what made the faith of Mary, eternal diamond, because it was absolutely relentless, and yet crystallized into what Yeats would call a terrible beauty.

We began talking about Isabel, and the way her life was determined by the sickness of her mother. What the example shows is that certain sufferings are more than just a question of time and special circumstances. Some are destinies. So it was with Isabel and the sad loneliness that her life always included.

And so, too, with Mary. The next time you have a chance to pray, try to have a dialogue with the Blessed Virgin about the secret of sharing the cross with Jesus.

Mary, can I walk with you a while? There is no need of words. I only want to accompany you. I pray that these steps I take with you will lead me on an inner journey. Amen.

THE SECOND SORROW

The Flight Into Egypt

In the Norton Simon Museum in Pasadena, California, hangs a painting by Italian Renaissance master Jacopo da Ponte called "Flight Into Egypt." The subject is a very traditional one, but da Ponte has two distinctive elements in his painting. The first is the extraordinary haste shown by the Holy Family, the donkey, and the angel that leads them. The flight is seen as it is communicated in the Scriptures — a race against death.

The technique of the painter is interesting. He shows Mary holding Christ on an animal obviously in motion. Joseph, his tunic tucked up by his knees, walks holding the slack rope attached to the donkey. The angel is running, arms outstretched, one foot on the ground, the other apparently in air. What really sets off all this motion is the fact that others in the picture are not moving. Three men and a dog are stationary. Their lack of movement contrasts with the haste of the Holy Family, and adds a note of symbolic indifference.

That indifference is the other distinctive element,

something more interesting than technique. It is symbolic. W.H. Auden, noting how many masterpieces have seemingly irrelevant scenes on the canvas alongside the scenes that most speak to our faith, understood this to be an insight. In his poem, "Musée des Beaux Artes," he explained this:

> About Suffering they were never wrong,
> The Old Masters: how well they understood
> Its human position; how it takes place
> While someone else is eating or opening a window
> or just walking dully along.

Tragedy happens while we are not aware of it. In da Ponte's picture, a drunkard imbibes as the Holy Family rush past to Egypt. He is near to the Lord and yet so far from him. In this he has something in common with us, for we, too, miss recognizing Jesus. Part of the complexity of our world is that we are so close to so much suffering, or at least have knowledge of it, and at the same time are so distanced from it — or at least so indifferent to it.

The Second Sorrow of Mary has to do with a suffering which we cannot help knowing about — that of so many refugees and displaced persons in the world. Around the globe, masses of humanity flee homelands sometimes with the hope of a better life and sometimes just of survival. Ours is becoming a world of refugees. Jesus, Mary, and Joseph were also refugees. The harsh fate of a woman refugee — trying to make a home, trying to get food for the family, doing all the traditional and very difficult tasks of washing and mending clothes with primitive techniques

— this was also the fate of the Queen of Heaven and Earth. When I was in Nairobi, Kenya, I noticed the great number of Somalis in the city, which is like a magnet for poor and oppressed people of Eastern Africa. There are Sudanese, Ugandans, Somalis, many of whom walk over a thousand miles to reach what they hope will be a haven. The slums of Nairobi offer them some safety at least. The Somalis look and dress differently from the residents of Nairobi. Their women wear flowing robes and veils that are like the traditional clothes that Mary wears in most artistic representations. There is an elegance about the Somalis, a lightness to their thin bodies that belies the sad reality of the history which explains their presence in Nairobi. Before all else, they can consider their survival against the odds as a tremendous achievement.

Naturally, they face the problems of all unwanted immigrants. Where are the poor welcome? Sometimes the best that they can hope for is an indifferent tolerance. They make their lives in the presence of everyone but at the same time on the margin of everything.

I saw Mary among the Somalis on the corners of Nairobi's downtown. She had the look of weariness past mere fatigue. The relentlessness of life on the run had etched itself into her thin face. Her eyes, nervous about the traffic, saw sorrows I could only imagine. Here I am, she seemed to say to me, with these poor refugees.

How modern the Second Sorrow of the Virgin Mary! She knew flight, she passed the hardship of exile. The precariousness of life was made obvious to her as it has rarely or never been for us in America. The grace hidden in the sufferings of so many poor women in the world — Haitians, Vietnamese boat-people, Bosnians, Sudanese — is the silent compassion of Christ and his mother, a compassion that says, "We too."

Jesus' exile was in some way political, just like the many poor who are political refugees of our time. The Gospel of St. Matthew is certainly not a political text, but it is clear that the birth of Our Lord was seen as subversive by the powers that were. In St. Matthew there is no pause for the shepherds or even the Presentation in the Temple, both of which we know about only from St. Luke's Gospel. Instead, we immediately go to the Epiphany, the manifestation to the nations represented by the Magi, and its ominous message of the threat to the life of the child.

It would be well for us to read the brief account, attentive to some of its nuances:

> Now when Jesus was born in Bethlehem of Judea in the days of Herod the king, behold, wise men from the East came to Jerusalem, saying, "Where is he who has been born king of the Jews? For we have seen his star in the East, and have come to worship him." When Herod the king heard this, he was troubled, and all Jerusalem with him; and assembling all the chief priests and scribes of the people, he inquired of them where the Christ was to be born.

They told him, "In Bethlehem of Judea; for so it is written by the prophet:
'And you, O Bethlehem, in the land of Judah,
are by no means least among the rulers of Judah;
for from you shall come a ruler who will govern my people Israel.' "

Then Herod summoned the wise men secretly and ascertained from them what time the star appeared; and he sent them to Bethlehem, saying, "Go and search diligently for the child, and when you have found him bring me word, that I too may come and worship him." When they had heard the king they went their way; and lo, the star which they had seen in the East went before them, till it came to rest over the place where the child was. When they saw the star, they rejoiced exceedingly with great joy; and going into the house they saw the child with Mary his mother, and they fell down and worshiped him. Then, opening their treasures, they offered him gifts, gold, frankincense and myrrh. And being warned in a dream not to return to Herod, they departed to their own country by another way.

Now when they had departed, behold, an angel of the Lord appeared to Joseph in a dream and said, "Rise, take the child and his mother, and flee to Egypt, and remain there till I tell you; for Herod is about to search for the child, to destroy him." And he rose and took the child and his mother by night, and departed to Egypt, and remained there until the death of Herod (RSV Mt 2:1-15).

The devotion of the Seven Sorrows is a biblical Marian prayer. The relationship between Mary and Jesus is at the center. We grow in our understanding of Mary's discipleship by nourishing ourselves with the word of God. Our relationship with her deepens our connection with her Son, who is the Word.

Clearly, the first thing to be noticed is the contrast between kings and cities. Jesus is associated with Bethlehem. Bethlehem had been the birthplace of King David and was held to be the place where the Messiah (who was to be a "Son" of David) would be born. St. Matthew begins his Gospel with the genealogy which demonstrates that Jesus was of the lineage of David. Thus, he was the true king. Herod is the usurper, and it is not surprising that his being troubled upsets his capital city also. The Magi seek the king of the Jews. Herod thought he was the king of the Jews, but was not of the blessed royal line. He was the descendant of an Idumean, the Greco-Roman name for the country of the Bible's Edomites, and a Nabatean Arab woman. Although Jewish by religious practice, he was an outsider. As a tyrant, whose way to the throne had been liberally washed in blood, he was always insecure.

The birth of Jesus was of course subversive to Satan, the prince of this world, and to the reign of sin, but the evangelist says that the reigning monarch felt threatened, also. It was an evil regime. Herod was a brutal tyrant whose thirty-three years of power were painted in blood, even the blood of his own family members.

He was a man who killed his brother-in-law to seal his security on the throne, and then killed a wife, and, finally, even his own sons. The emperor Augustus was reported to have said that he would rather be Herod's pig than his son. Herod obeyed the kosher laws so the pig was safe, but three of the king's sons were not. They were executed. This was an unjust man who worried about the sign of the birth of the new king. Herod was an astute politician who knew how to keep himself in power. Through machinations and an alliance with Antony and Cleopatra, Herod had been named "King of the Jews" by the Roman Senate. He was a *rex socius*, an allied king, and thus dependent on imperial approbation and support. He had some serious setbacks, like being on the wrong side against

Augustus, but somehow he always knew how to recoup. He was extremely crafty.

Herod's duplicity in the Gospel is quite in character. He says nothing about his evil intentions for the child. He actually masks his intent to murder in false piety. He says that he wants to pay homage to the child himself, as if he were the new king's regent instead of rival. The passage about Herod is a thumbnail sketch of evil even before we hear about the Slaughter of the Innocents.

The greater part of the evils of humanity are inflicted by humans. Jesus, Mary, and Joseph fleeing from an oppressive tyrant should remind us of the present-day Herods whose wicked selfishness is the source of so much injustice and violence. Governments which should be dedicated to the common good instead dedicate themselves to helping the rich get richer, to the restriction of basic freedoms, and the destruction of human life.

Mary was a victim of injustice, as are the women in refugee camps all around the globe. There is something terribly current about the Second Sorrow. Mary, model of the Church, in her flight into Egypt, revealed a sacred dimension about the life of the refugee. The politics of her time made the life of the poor perilous. And so she fled with her child.

Divine intervention foils Herod's plans. The Magi are warned not to trust the false king of Jerusalem in order to protect the vulnerable young king they worshiped. Joseph, a holy dreamer, receives yet another message in a dream to take "the child and his mother" to safety. They are warned, but they still have to run for their lives. Thousands of people are in the same position today. If only we could feel the desperate terror which affects so many! A baby had something to fear from the evil in the heart of Herod. As I mentioned, St. Bernard said that the passion of Christ began with his birth. Certainly this is evident in the somber intimations that attend the birth of Jesus in the Gospel of St. Matthew. The myrrh which the Magi present to the infant king perhaps refers to death. The substance was used to prepare bodies for burial. Its well-known bitterness was a kind of prophecy. Herod's plot against Jesus certainly indicates the ominous fate of this child.

The English historian Macaulay, who was the apologist of the so-called Glorious Revolution whereby William of Orange usurped the throne of his father-in-law King James II, has an interesting passage about the birth of James II's son. The birth of the boy, who would later be called the Old Pretender, was a decisive event in the history of the Protestant-Catholic conflict in English history.

James II had two Protestant daughters when he assumed the throne of England upon the death of his brother Charles II. These daughters represented to some of the Protestants a type of insurance that the throne was only temporarily in the hands of a Roman Catholic. However, James II remarried after his wife died. His new wife gave birth to a male heir who then had the advantage over his half-sisters, Mary, the wife of William of Orange, and her sister Anne (who would eventually be queen).

The strange rivalry for the English throne was complicated by the fact that William of Orange was both son-in-law and nephew to James II. William's wife was his first cousin, his father-in-law his uncle. William considered himself an heir to the throne and attempted briefly to question the circumstances of his new cousin's birth. Eventually, William gained a king's crown, but not without a civil war and an insecurity about future challenges to the throne by his new cousin's son, Bonnie Prince Charlie.

Macaulay saw the fighting of the Stuart loyalists against the Protestant usurpers as an English tragedy. This is how he described the birth of the Catholic heir to the throne: "There, on the morning of Sunday, the tenth of June, a day long kept sacred by the too faithful adherents of a bad cause, was born the most unfortunate of princes, destined to seventy-seven years of exile and wandering, of vain projects, of honours more galling than insults, and of hopes such as make the heart sick."

The description is stirring for me because of the thought of the prince doomed from the cradle. Jesus was also in some respects, a most unfortunate prince, one without a palace, without power or possessions. His reign was associated with violence from the start. The first adherents for his cause died so that his enemy would not continue to seek him out. They were children like him, holy and innocent.

All his life Jesus lived under the threat of a violent death. The ancient Greeks told the story of the sword that hung above Damocles' head to remind him of the fragility of his power. Jesus lived with the threat of destruction from the beginning. And that means that Mary, his mother, was implicated from the beginning in the fatal character of his future. This indicates that we too have some share in the "hopes such as make the heart sick," the embattled hopes of the Gospel.

I served in El Salvador from January 1986 to July

1993. The country was at war for six of those years, until a peace settlement was more or less imposed by the United States in 1992. They were interesting years to say the least. The failed revolution in that country was like an earthquake that changed the human shape of the country. In my parish, we had many people who came from different parts of the country, most of them fleeing the violence that hit some sections more than others. In them could be seen the image of the Holy Family escaping to Egypt.

Some of them came without much of anything. The possessions of the poor are so often tragically eloquent. Some clothes, pots and dishes that represent the necessary tools of living, plastic bags with papers, religious objects, trinkets — fragments of a life.

The awful nature of the refugee experience makes me want to make it as concrete as possible for the reader. Imagine this: Tell a middle class American that, in order to survive, he or she must leave at night carrying all that he or she owns. How many would survive a journey of just one week?

When they arrive at their destination tired and homesick, point out a hill like the one outside the town where I served as pastor. No plumbing, a steep incline, no building materials. Say to them: "You can stay here, with the wonderful view of the ocean and the restaurants frequented by the rich on the beach. You may look at such a world, but that is all. The most you can hope for is a job cleaning such places, and you will be happy for such a job.

"Do something about an outhouse, never mind the hostility of the *señora* whose house is close by; neither she nor her husband the colonel really can say anything to you.

We will give you some two-by-fours and some pieces of corrugated metal. Build a home with sticks and mud, bricks if you can get them. Eventually, we will string up some posts so that every house can have an electric outlet and a naked bulb hanging over the dirt floor of the house."

I lived close to the people who inhabited that very hill. I visited their sick, and on one traumatic and memorable occasion, helped carry a lady down the hill on a rainy night so that she could get to the hospital.

But I still cannot believe the rigor of such poverty, the scraping so close to the edge of human ability to survive. What is it like living when nothing can be assumed, not light in the twelve hours of darkness, not refrigerators to take out something easy to make for supper, not even water if someone doesn't go down to the *pila* (water faucet) to bring it to the house?

All these things that I wonder at were part of Mary's life. The Flight into Egypt, with all the beautiful art that it has inspired, was something not at all beautiful. It was a matter of survival — a pressing to the limits of endurance.

I knew a family that fled the houses near a great bridge in El Salvador. The bridge was blown up by the guerrillas in a move that was intended to divide the country in half. Although the military scheme did not work, a great deal of inconvenience was produced. Even now, as I write this in 1997, the bridge over the river Lempa has yet to be rebuilt and cars crossing the river must use an old train bridge.

There were poor houses along the road leading up to the bridge. Were they from the time when the bridge workers were still there? Had they been houses of the poor who cooked the food for the workers? I do not know. People cluster where there is hope of work; that much of economics I learned in the Third World.

The army had been taken by surprise when the bridge blew up. The bombing must have taken a good deal of explosives, and naturally the army suspected that the people who lived close by must have had some sort of idea of what was going on before the great explosion. The military threw people out of their houses; men were arrested and never seen again. The war, as I said, was a constant earthquake. One young man I knew never recovered from the naked fear that his life was in danger from the soldiers. He told me the story with a voice rough with emotion.

Families migrated to where they had relatives or friends, and sometimes just to the opposite compass point from danger. Sometimes their only capital was a bag of corn, some chickens, the energy with which they would work. It was hardest on the babies, of course, but it was difficult for everyone.

This was just one case, but I think of it because of the suddenness of Joseph's revelation. "That very night the journey began," the Scripture says. For these people it was the same — a terrible explosion, and life as they knew it was over.

The word used for such people in El Salvador was *desplazados* — the displaced. All of us have the need to be rooted somewhere, to feel that "here I fit in." The displaced lack that sense of connectedness. They cannot easily feel that they are "at home." Home is a place that is far away.

Mary, the Mother of Sorrows, knew the feeling of displacement, of uprootedness, the insecurity of not being within a familiar frame of reference that feels like something of the family. Mary was a *desplazada*.

Egypt had a large Jewish colony in the first century. There was even a Jewish temple at Leontopolis, which, regarded as schismatic in Jerusalem, was presided over by a priest from the Zadokite high-priestly line. There was a high Jewish culture in Egypt. The famous Septuagint translation of the Old Testament was the Greek version of the Hebrew which was apparently already a little remote for the Hellenized Egyptian Jews.

There is a famous French novel titled *Abraham* by Marek Halter which follows Jewish history from the destruction of Herod's Temple to after the Nazi Holocaust. An interesting chapter of the book describes the life of a family of Jewish refugees in Alexandria. Abraham, who stays with his uncle, finds the cosmopolitan and grand city of Alexandria quite alienating. How can life continue and lose itself in business and daily pleasures when Jerusalem has been destroyed?

The Gospel of St. Matthew does not explore the possibilities of experience contained within the mentioned exile in Egypt. Evidently, the evangelist is really more interested in associating a Scripture quote, "Out of Egypt I have called my son," than anything else. Considering the number of people in this world living away from their homeland, some meditation on the life of the exiled as it relates to Christ and his blessed Mother is useful.

Like Israel, the evangelist says Jesus knew what it was to be a stranger in a strange land. Like Israel, Jesus was brought to the Promised Land. That return indicates a parallel with the Passover, but it also represents a homecoming, a reconciling. The alienation of Egypt gives way to the true homeland. For our purpose, meditating on the

Sorrows of Mary, what strikes us is the association of the Mother of God with so many who have lived the alienation of being uprooted by fear.

An old Cuban song says that the homeland can hurt you when you are far away. Here we are not talking about a temporary homesickness, but something like a desperation. Since my return to the States from the missions, I have felt an overpowering sensation of loss and disconnectedness. This has made me sensitive to the Latin Americans whom I have encountered here in the States. I imagine that Mary felt like some of them, far away from family and friends, cut off from the spiritual resources that were once so much more accessible.

Some of the *desplazados* I knew in El Salvador were the most religious people I worked with; others lost their faith or were weakened in it because of the loss of familiar supports. That is why, in my opinion, Mary must be a big part of the American Church's pastoral care for Hispanics, because she can be a focus for understanding how faith can grow even away from home.

The Second Sorrow has taken us far afield, across both geography and history, but it should have taken us even further, on a journey inward. You and I must accompany Mary on the Flight into Egypt.

The night is chill; the only familiar sounds are those of our own haste. Other sounds may even frighten us. Deadly hatred is at our heels. The world is an unstable place, and almost all that we counted on as our own is revealed to be both fragile and impossible to hold.

Deeper into the night we go, with only what we can carry. Our only security is our destination away from harm.

We cannot think about tomorrow or its troubles, what we will we eat or where we will rest. Sufficient is the hard path we walk this night. God is protecting us, but meanwhile, life as we know it has come to an end. We leave so much behind. Fear gnaws at our stomach.

Like Joseph, we must be strong. Like Mary, we need to hang on to Jesus. That embrace will be our only security.

Concentrate on the scene in your own mind. Try to feel all that the situation implies. And then say something like this to your mother:

Mary, teach us to be free like you, free to leave behind what we do not need.

Mary, teach us to be strong like you, strong to carry Christ with us, to make a home for him wherever we might be.

Mary, teach us compassion for so many, especially poor women, who suffer so much because of this world's unrest. Amen.

THE THIRD SORROW

The Finding in the Temple

She had always had a hard time convincing him that he was sick enough to go to the hospital. He had always wanted to stay at home; he had hated the hospital. It was strange that in the last hours of life he begged them to take him to Bloom Hospital.

The irony of it must have been difficult. *"No, mi hijo, vas a estar mejor aqui,"* which means, "My son, it will be better for you here." She knew no hospital could save him now. This final part of the journey, he was better off at home.

She held him in her arms as he died, a *pietà* with Christ still in his pajamas. He trembled as his spirit wrestled free. She rocked him, soothed him, spoke to him, while she prayed to God that the agony be over.

Like so many poor women, denied access to education, she was wise in the things of the heart. She knew that her son would die with the same assurance she knew that it would soon be dawn.

I think of her in that scene. It was still before dawn, and there was a chill in the air. The light bulb over the cement sink lit the place she and her boy sat. He coughed blood, and she could only hold him closer to herself. His words about wishing to go to the hospital, which he had always hated, cut straight to her heart. Now that there was no hope, the boy had decided to go to the hospital. Obviously the twelve-year-old knew that this time death was very near. He was instinctively seeking some kind of an escape.

When she spoke to me about this last scene in a tragically-short life, I misread the cues badly. I thought that she was feeling guilty that there had been no desperate last run to the hospital in San Salvador, an hour's trip which he would not have survived. Surely, I said to her, you know that you did everything you could.

She knew that she had. We had moved heaven and earth to try to save the boy, even begging a man in the Knights of Columbus who worked in the embassy to help us by getting medicine from the U.S. Our hearts had been broken in the grinding process of the boy's death.

The mother had no need of reassurance. I assumed that I would have to justify "the ways of God to man," to use Milton's phrase. Priests are sometimes asked to do impossible things, and sometimes we put ourselves in the stew. What the woman wanted was simply someone who would just listen to her and acknowledge how bitter the chalice was that she had to drink.

From the beginning, she had had a terrible feeling about how things would end. Everyone told her that that was ridiculous, that she should have faith and never give up hope. Eventually, she convinced herself of the necessity of hope. She, too, had started to believe.

Less sophisticated people often have more stories to tell about premonitions and intuitions. I have become a believer in prophetic intuition myself. Some people have special gifts, and sometimes there are moments and signs which really do indicate a path to us. Sometimes, the subconscious recognizes things the conscious mind does not. How many stories of saints indicate an extraordinary irony? How many times do ironic details, even in history, seem so fantastic that they would be rejected in fiction?

Maria, for that is what we shall call her, had always had a fear about her children. This fear, for whatever reason, made her give Juan repeated blood tests. With one came the diagnosis she had dreaded so much yet seemed to expect. The boy had leukemia.

Leukemia kills children even in the United States. What chance did Juan have in a poor town in El Salvador? It is painful for me even to think of the history of the disease and its fatal progress in the child's body.

It was like a journey to another world for me. Until that time, I had known only the rural area of El Salvador where I was a pastor of a parish, and the places of San Salvador, the capital, which were part of the gringo itinerary — government offices, the archdiocesan offices, the chapel where Archbishop Romero was killed saying Mass, his grave beneath the cathedral, and a few other sites where gringos and rich Salvadorans could relax. Through Juan, I was introduced to another side of the country — the national health-care system.

The Babies and Children's Hospital of the country was badly damaged by the 1986 earthquake. It had been relocated to a compound of buildings hastily built or converted to care for the most vulnerable of the poor of El Salvador — sick children whose parents had no means.

In that hospital, children die every day. There was at the time a *funeraria* right across the street from the hospital's gates that sold small caskets, the smallest made of styrofoam. Some parents would wait outside the place for relatives to come to help them to pay for the narrow boxes, which would very often then be loaded atop a bus for the sad journeys home.

From the start we had little hope that Juan would survive. But we took consolation in telling ourselves, "They have caught it in time." There were moments of seeming triumph. A transfusion seemed to work wonders; a new medicine put him in remission; the doctors were cautiously optimistic. Hope against hope, until gradually leaf after leaf fell from the tree, and winter came.

Another memory comes to me. Again Juan was in the hospital, but this time he was not in the Babies and Children's Hospital but in a local public-health facility. He was in the bed, pale and tired, the weak eye of an emotional storm that had engulfed his parents. His father could not handle this child's illness. It was so wrong to him that he withdrew into resentment of God. I was there with both mother and father, wondering what to say, as usual. Somewhere deep in my childhood there must have been some trauma that makes me feel that words will materialize in any given trouble and make everything better, and that their expression depends on me.

The couple was going through a tough time. At that point, the two of them were intimately linked by the suffering of their child, but not by understanding. How many women have I known whose husbands did not have a clue about what really moved or pained their wives? How many marriages were made, not so much out of convenience but of something much worse — necessity. A man and a woman can be together but really be so far apart emotionally. A relationship based on pity and even a sort of tenderness is not the covenant of love we hope to see in marriage.

We were in the hospital when I took some of this in. As we were leaving, we met a woman in the corridor from our same town. She happened to be there visiting a friend or relative. She was quite a strong person, someone who had been involved in politics and community organizing. Such strong women in Latin countries are typically godmother to countless children and are the fixers and natural leaders for many others.

She immediately started asking questions. What had been done so far? How old was the boy? What had the doctors said? Had they gone to any other hospital? Her experience had taught her to be what is called "proactive" today. Without some exertion of energy, she knew that children could die quickly. "And do not neglect your husband and your other sons," she said quickly to the woman. She picked up on the husband's despair in a mere glance and was not afraid to speak to it.

Maria was inconsolable, however. It was very astute of this woman to identify the need to watch the husband and even to talk about the other children, even though it was impossible. There is an inevitability to some human disasters that seems as irresistible as geology. We could not stop them even if we had enough awareness to want to do so.

It was probably more than year later when Juan

died in his mother's arms. But Maria had seen it coming long before. She had seen it that day in the corridor. Her premonition had not impeded her from fighting the good fight, though she had shown the strength, not out of conviction, but because of the others. She thought her lack of faith was terrible, even sinful. No one could have thought that she doubted the value of all that time and effort.

I certainly was fooled. She would frequently come to talk to me. I would search for words, because I didn't know what else I could do. There were things that we could occasionally help with, rides to the doctor and to the hospital. Through the boy's sad decline, I worried that Maria would not survive the cruel blow of the child's death. I dared not tell her to prepare herself for fear of alienating her all the more.

Only in retrospect do I recognize that there was a story I was missing. Why was I still in the hospital corridor in some way? How did I miss the signs of a grief that was anticipated like that of David's for his first son by Bathsheba? Maria had lived with the death of her boy a long time before it happened.

What has all this to do with the Third Sorrow of Mary, "The Finding in the Temple?" No doubt you have anticipated me in this, but let us read what the Scripture says of this incident before we reflect further. The text is from the second chapter of St. Luke, verses 41-52:

> Each year his parents went
> to Jerusalem for the feast of the
> Passover, and when he was
> twelve years old, they went up

according to festival custom. After they had completed its days, as they were returning, the boy Jesus remained behind in Jerusalem, but his parents did not know it. Thinking that he was in the caravan, they journeyed for a day and looked for him among their friends and acquaintances, but not finding him, they returned to Jerusalem to look for him. After three days, they found him in the temple, sitting in the midst of the teachers, listening to them and asking them questions, and all who heard him were astounded at his understanding and his answers. When his parents saw him, they were astonished, and his mother said to him, "Son, why have you done this to us? Your father and I have been looking for you with great anxiety." And he said to them, "Why were you looking for me? Did you not know that I must be in my Father's house?" But they did not understand what he said to them. He went down with them then, and

came to Nazareth, and was obe-
dient to them; and his mother
kept all these things in her
heart. And Jesus advanced [in]
wisdom and age and favor before
God and man.

The reading is very familiar, but we will remember
something the German philosopher Heidegger said in his
book *Introduction to Metaphysics*: "In everything well-
known something worthy of thought still lurks." We need
to approach familiar Scripture readings with fresh energy
in order to see the "deep-down freshness" there.

In the case of this reading, I do not recall ever associating the Finding in the Temple with the story of the
Resurrection. Yet there are clear indications of similarity.
Christ is discovered on the third day of his parents' search.
A separation is followed by an enigmatic reunion. Mary
and Joseph do not understand any more than the apostles
understood what was happening when Christ appeared to
them after rising from the dead. The apostles would need
Pentecost to shift gears; this reading tells us only that Mary
"kept all these things in her heart."

St. Alphonsus, writing about this Sorrow of Mary,
mentions that some authors thought that it was the most
intensely sad of all seven. This was because in all the other
Sorrows, Mary had the consolation of close physical prox-
imity with Jesus. In this case, the Sorrow included separation. The great Greek Father Origen said that the anxiety
of Joseph and Mary was the thought that Jesus "had entirely left them."

For the Fathers of the Church, as well as for others who wrote about this Sorrow, the Virgin Mother's search for her son in Jerusalem was symbolic of our seeking of the Lord. Origen wrote, "Learn, then, from Mary to seek Jesus." That leads to the house of the Father of Jesus. The rediscovery of Christ is a theme that is worthy of meditation. Especially, this applies to us sinners. We have lost the company of Jesus, and then we are able to regain it. How many times have we prayed the joyful mysteries and yet not ever personalized the idea of search and reencounter?

This Sorrow, then, can be taken as a model of conversion. We should never forget that our conversion is a process which should never stop. The greatest of saints were convinced that they were the greatest of sinners. Their humility should warn us away from self-complacency. When we fall into patterns that indicate self-righteousness, like judging others without charity, we need to recall that we will only find Jesus again in his Father's house, or, as some translations have it, doing the Father's business. The business is usually about that which we are insufficiently busy.

I must confess, however, that my reaction to this Sorrow of Mary has a different focus. The three days of separation and search are clearly spiritually symbolic, but what interests me more is what happened afterward.

That is why I compare Mary with this Maria. For me, the Finding in the Temple was the beginning of a sorrow that had to last all of Mary's life. That sorrow was the knowledge that her ideas about her Son had to be revised constantly in terms of this "business of His Father."

The sadness of so many mothers is that their best

hopes for their children are frustrated. Obviously, sometimes these hopes are ill-founded, but that cannot negate the love that inspires them. This Sorrow for me is about the frustration of Mary's hopes for her Child.

St. Luke makes a point of Mary's ongoing meditation on the incident by saving for last the comment "And his mother kept all these things in her heart." Certainly, there is a clue here for all of us. The point of the story is that Mary could not have ordinary expectations. She could expect only disappointment. What was going to happen to this child? Mary's mind had to go back to Simeon's prophecy and recall the sword that lurked in her future.

The great thing of life in the Lord is the discovery of the contrast between our will — our wants and desires — and the divine will. The Finding in the Temple indicates that Mary was aware of this contrast between what she wanted and God's will. This Third Sorrow begs for a solution like Jesus' words in the garden; "Not my will, but thine be done." Evidently this could have been part of Mary's meditation.

The poignancy that we associate with Mary's search for Jesus refers to profound events in our lives. What happens when what we hope for the people we love cannot come true? Many would rather suffer themselves than see their loved ones suffer. What disturbs us more than the suffering or death of children? It goes against the grain of our nature.

Once I concelebrated the funeral Mass of a priest I had known since the first years of my priesthood. He had died of cancer and the painful progress of the disease whittled him down to a shadow of his former self before he died. His funeral was well-attended because he had been well-liked. Many of his brother priests were there, both from his religious order and from the presbyterate of the diocese.

One mourner stood out for me. The priest's mother, another Mary, was ninety years old and sat in the first pew. The auxiliary bishop of the diocese spoke some words after Communion and addressed them mostly to her. The message was quite moving, especially since the bishop himself was obviously moved.

"Mary," said the bishop, "something very special has happened here. It is unusual that a child leaves a legacy to a parent, yet your son left you a legacy, not one that can be evaluated by accountants, but a legacy of great value nonetheless." The tremendous irony of a ninety-year-old mother attending the funeral of her son was very moving. Who could not be impressed with the silent bravery of the old woman? Her nods of agreement to the bishop, who looked at her with real sympathy, were more eloquent even than his words.

In this Third Sorrow, I see the irony of the Blessed Virgin's life summarized and anticipated. There would come a day when she would mourn this son. She had to feel that somehow in her heart. She had to know that she would survive him. That is why I think of Maria with the awful sensation she had that day in the hospital corridor. The fatal impression that the battle was already lost. Or, maybe not the battle, because there were battles that seemed victorious, but the whole war lost. There have been battles recorded in history in which exceptionally brave men have fought only to learn afterwards that it was all in vain, that the war was over and their scars superfluous. There are such battles in the lives of many. It requires a special sort of courage to continue efforts that seem doomed.

I think that Mary showed an analogous courage in her perseverance despite her consciousness that inevitably she would have to give Jesus up, offer him back to his Father. Maria sensed what Mary did. That is the point of this comparison. Both mothers of twelve-year-old boys, both with a terrible sense of the fragility of the life of those whom they love, the constant danger that could ambush any of us. Leukemia claimed Maria's son within a few years. Mary's son lived a much longer time than that, but every precious moment of that time was somehow colored by the shadows that lurked ahead.

Both women needed courage to carry on. Both shared intense communion with their sons. The attachment between the two involved almost a fusion. After the prolonged illness and death of someone close to us, we miss even the work we once dreaded, the time spent in doctors' offices or in the car, the visits to the hospital, the difficult tasks of attention. We identified so much with the person that our new freedom finds us sullen and lost. Whereas once we pleaded for more time to do things, we now feel lost and cannot fill up the time. Our communion meant that these aspects of the life of the loved one became aspects of our life. Somehow we were one.

That oneness is what we celebrate in the Virgin Mary and her relationship to her Son Jesus. Certainly it was a source of tremendous joy to Mary, but was also the cause of grief. Grace almost always comes with a grief; the crown is connected with the cross. Maria's crown is not as evident as the cross. Naturally, an experience so hard leaves some traces. But she can always feel that the bond she had with her son, in its intensity and its beauty, was a sign of God's suffering love. It was an image of another mother's love for her Son, something that was demonstrated till the last moment before peace prevailed in her child's life.

All of us, if pressed, could name some person we know who suffered something tragic like the death of a child. We need to get beyond even sympathy in our meditation on this Sorrow. We must actually *embrace* its message that God's will may contrast with ours.

Once I attended a conference in which all of us were asked to write down on slips of paper three things that were precious to us: a favorite place; a special ambition; a person we loved very much. The exercise was about Abraham and how the Lord had asked him to give up so much. When we got to the point of listening to the sacrifice of Isaac, we were told to "give up" that special person to God, even if it meant that we would never see him or her again. People groaned at the idea, but it was a wonderful way to think about the faith of Abraham and the sacrifice asked of him. Can we imagine a choice so cruel as between our love of God and our wanting to be close to someone we love with deep and unselfish love?

Maybe you have already learned this lesson. I can imagine nothing more searing. I lost a little nephew, and the pain of the loss still affects the family. It is puzzling, this contrast between what we think is best and what God wills. It can stun you and hurt you. And it has to be something for us to take to heart in the manner of Mary, which I am sure was a kind of prayer.

With very intuitive people, a hint is enough. Really

sharp people can take things in on the first try, something that is a lot harder for those of us who come to awareness gradually. The saints often show a wonderful intuition, a deep insight into the shape of God's grace in our lives.

This Sorrow was like a hint of the deepest current of the life of Jesus — his commitment to the will of the Father. I am sure Mary well understood its import. The brilliant need only the sketchiest of directions in order to find their way to deep thoughts. Mary's spiritual brilliance enabled her to get to the definition of the problem. She did not need another hint in her life. I am sure this Sorrow has much to teach us. First, let us share in the anxiety of Mary and Joseph, an anxiety that involves the separation from Jesus, whom we love.

Then let us see that a simple incident and a dialogue with few words was really a tremendous sign of the future. Did Jesus tell us that he was not walking with us because he was about something else, the affairs of his Father, the things of "his Father's house"?

When you feel that Jesus is no longer in your company, you must imitate Mary and go looking for him. You are bound to find him in the temple. His response to your pain may seem to be cold, but is really the greatest gentleness. He wants you to know the truth that sets us free. His love for you is within a greater love which gives it meaning that is eternal, but which does not permit internal contradictions to get in the way. It is either the will of his Father, or it is something harmful.

That does not make it easy. Choices are often difficult, and our poor hearts feel ambushed at times. Clarity is a great thing, but it is precious because it is so costly.

Our Mother Mary had a great clarity in her life. We are meditating on her model of discipleship and need to put our hearts first to understand the crucial trials of her life. "Great love means great pain," as the ancients said. If we would love greatly, there is an inevitable corollary.

Lord, I am so unlike your mother. She was so quick to learn your will, and I am so slow. Teach me, as you taught her great heart, but be patient with me. I know it will take me a long time to catch on, and, besides, I am so weak. Give me the consolation of the love of your mother. With her I will learn to seek you out in your Father's house; with her, I will learn acceptance. Amen.

THE FOURTH SORROW

Jesus Meets His Mother on the Way to Calvary

Sometimes poverty is actually a help to piety. This is not to justify the terrible conditions so many live under which really are the fruit of injustice. It is simply a fact of experience that many missionaries who have worked with the poor can understand. Materialism chokes the seed of the word as shown in the Gospel parable of the Sower. People who have little to distract them can get enthusiastic about the things of the Lord.

In El Salvador, poor and war-torn, the popularity of all-night prayer vigils in our parish and others was partially explained by the absence of other activities. When we started celebrating vigils of Eucharistic Adoration in our parish, we had surprising success. The monotony of the campesino's life, the belief in the power of prayer, the exhilaration of singing all night, the great sense of community that Salvadorans have, their respect for a cherished tradition — all these things combined to make the vigils a religious experience.

We began with a Mass and ended with a Mass. All

night long there were Rosaries, hymns, reflections, Bible readings, and confessions. And more confessions. The night, the emotion, the prayer, all provoked an intense response. As I heard so many people's failures and frustrations, wave after wave of feelings broke over me. It was like being on the shore of life and the energy of an ocean of troubles was coming at me.

One vigil took place on a rainy night. The chapel was a shell — a wooden frame and a roof — and the confessional was a spot under a tree. The original idea was that I would hear the penitents at the side of the altar on which the Blessed Sacrament was exposed. But the confidentiality of the penitent would suffer in the arrangement, as would my nerves, from the strain of trying to hear what was being said through the drone of the prayers, the enthusiastic singing, and the thunder of the pouring rain on the roof of the chapel.

And so, the confessional beneath the tree. Besides the branches of the tree, both I and the penitent had an umbrella to protect us from the rain. The passing of the umbrella was the signal for each new confession. There is a picturesque quality to life in the missions of which I confess I am fonder now that it is only remembered and not lived.

One particular confession of that long rainy night has stayed in my mind. A very good woman, who had come a great distance to pray, spent a good deal of time reviewing her life with me.

I think she told me of every defeat she had felt in her life. This included her mother's suspicions when she was a young girl, the disappointment of her marriage, and all the problems she had had with her nine children. They had moved several times, something you cannot appreciate without having seen how poor people in Salvador set up a new place to live — with walls of sticks and mud and pieces of sheet metal for the roof. Then there is the search for water to drink and to wash the laundry, the rhythm of a hard, pioneering life without electricity most of the time, without access to medical care, and sometimes without schools.

I suppose most Americans would admire her for her incredible toughness. Such people endure what seems impossible to us, and yet there is a simplicity and sensitivity to them that is also incredible. I have talked to many an illiterate woman who knew so much more of life than I who have had so many advantages. Experience taught them and intuition guided them to a deep compassion. Obviously some were profoundly limited by their experiences, with little imagination or flexibility. Lack of education, a brutal life, a horizon that holds little but hard physical work — these all take their toll. But there were some wonders: women whose memory continues to inspire me about the indomitable nature of the human spirit.

Let us call this woman Monica. The name comes to mind because of her long-suffering motherhood. In words that were as simple as they were emotionally devastating, Monica told me of her sufferings with her two sons.

The first got involved with the guerrillas and was killed in a skirmish with soldiers. People who have not lived in desperate parts of the Third World cannot hope to understand the appeal of Marxist revolutionaries. I was no missionary enthralled with what I called the false god of revolution; nevertheless, I could see that for many the question had nothing to do with communism at all. To some young men motivated by a burning sense of injustice, the Marxists seemed to be the only alternative. Some of these young men, and young women, were first active in the Church. Their leadership skills and their commitment to the welfare of their neighbors was precisely what revolutionary leaders were looking for.

It was a nation's tragedy that so many idealistic young people were sacrificed in the violence that beset El Salvador for more than a decade. Progress was arrested, innocent victims suffered tremendously, callous manipulation and brutality were the order of the day. I really think most people did not even want to take a side; they wanted only some way to live through the turbulence.

Monica's family life indicated how people could suffer in such a conflict. Her eldest son killed by soldiers, a younger son became a soldier. This war was not like our Civil War where brothers sometimes were on opposite sides because of ideological positions. Most who served in the Salvadoran Army did so without volunteering. Drafting included impressment of young men who were standing on the street corners in country towns. For the years of the war that I lived in La Libertad, there was only one skirmish in town, but every month pickup trucks would come looking for our youth.

One boy killed by soldiers, another son a soldier. The irony of the life of the poor in El Salvador is crushingly heavy. Monica somehow survived, praying to God to protect her son from boys like her other son who fought with the guerrillas. No doubt she prayed he would be protected but also that he would kill no one. I knew soldiers who told me that they prayed never to kill anyone when they were shooting, even in skirmishes.

Then the second son deserted, a not uncommon experience in El Salvador. Soldiers would go on leave and then never go back to base. The army really didn't have the means to control all of the cases, although sometimes young men ended up re-recruited. She no longer worried about whether her son would die fighting. Now she feared that he might die in prison if the authorities were able to get him.

She told me that he had an unstable character, one which led him to self-destructive behavior. I wish I could communicate the ups and downs of my emotion while she told me the story of her life. She did not anticipate anything in the story, so that I felt I was living through the death of the first son, then the military service of the second, then his desertion, then his finding a wife and building a home on some poor farmland somewhere. The mother had suffered through her sons. The narrative was about her union with her children in all their troubles. And this special son, the second, had carved a place in her heart in all his troubles. She felt more than anyone the danger he represented to himself.

Traveling was dangerous for him because the authorities could stop any bus anytime to check for identity papers. While she wanted to see him, she hoped that he would not come to see her. What she heard of his living arrangements — he had taken up with a young woman — and his continuous drinking, she was afraid for him. She sent him a message — she would try to go to see him. He should not endanger himself coming home to visit.

Of course, he came to the house. Naturally, he got to drinking and then got in a fight with both his father and a younger brother. She had to intervene, and he left to do some more drinking. What would happen to him? That night she couldn't sleep thinking of where he was, the inevitable way that trouble had of dogging his steps, the constant threat he was under thanks to the desertion.

In the morning, she was out of the hammock early as usual. A little away from the house, at the spring, she met her son. He just wanted to say goodbye to her. He was sheepish about the problems, and he didn't know about himself either. The meeting was like a drink of clear water for her thirsty heart. He understood her love for him, she was right to *regañar* (rebuke) him, and he said he was embarrassed by her tears.

She spoke about the problems she had, and her continued worry, but I could tell that in the chemistry of that early morning talk there had been consolation for her. Love without understanding is what Coleridge said about work without hope: it is nectar in a sieve. But there was at least some understanding. At least she knew that he had her love, and that was something to hold onto. Between the two, despite her disappointments and his deceptions, there was a solidarity. She would continue suffering and worrying, but at least she was able to share with someone the reality that their solidarity was something. Even if all the pieces in her life or in his never seemed to fit, there was this union of hearts.

It may seem strange to compare the Blessed Mother with a woman whose son was only trouble — really a cross she had to carry. The basis of my comparison is the imperfect but real solidarity between mother and son, and the mother's spiritual strength. The point is the tremendous spiritual strength of the woman; it reminded me of another mother and her solidarity with her Child.

A friend of mine went to Poland and upon his return gave me a wood carving of Jesus and Mary that I cherish very much. The carving is crude, the lines are simple. The art is not the reason why I care for the thing — the roughness communicates something and coordinates with its theme. The piece has Jesus carrying the cross and his mother walking beside him. She has her shoulder under part of the cross.

Mary as Simon of Cyrene? Doesn't that take liberties with the story the Gospels tell us? I think not. I think it expresses rather the mystical union of Mary and Jesus in his suffering. The sympathy she felt was total. In fact, sympathy is too weak a word; perhaps solidarity would be better.

Poland, whose beautiful Catholic faith blossoms on the bitter branches of the tree of her history, would naturally understand instinctively that Mary, too, shouldered the cross — not literally, but spiritually. The Church Fathers were wise about Mary's participation in the suffering of Jesus. St. Jerome commented, "Every wound inflicted on the body of Jesus was a wound in the heart of the Mother." Seeing her son carry the cross, this mother no doubt felt its weight.

This Sorrow is also the Fourth Station of the Cross. The Sorrows of Mary compaginate with other devotions because they have the same reference point — the life of Christ. All of the Sorrows are about the relationship between this particular mother and this particular Son. Everything that we know about Mary has to do with Christ. Union with Christ — that is the basic lesson of these Sorrows.

Mary is important to us especially because we want to imitate her in relationship to Christ. We cannot pretend to the privileged intimacy between two such grace-filled people, but we can try to evaluate our life in relationship to Christ. Everything known about us should reflect our relationship with Jesus Christ.

Mary's discipleship consisted of uniting her life with Christ's suffering. That identity is emphasized in the dramatic scene of mother and son on the way to Calvary. Like the bond between Monica and her son, sorrow constructs an encounter and implies an understanding.

Pious imagination has considered two aspects about the encounter. One is the mutual consolation of the two figures. No humans can be imagined closer in heart and soul. The other theme is one of recognition.

Jesus, because of the torture and mistreatment, was disfigured with suffering. Piety has often focused on the Servant prophecies of Isaiah with reference to the suffering Christ. "Even as many were amazed at him — so marred was his look beyond that of man," says Isaiah 52:14. Some who write about the Fourth Sorrow imagine that it is hard for the Virgin even to recognize Christ. Her love, however, sees beyond — to Christ who is underneath all innocent suffering. There is also, of course, recognition on the part of Jesus.

The symmetry of Christ and the Christian is one of the great messages of the devotion of the Seven Sorrows. What is said of Jesus is said of Mary, as it should be said of us. "The most sorrowful Mother," wrote St. Bernard, "meets her most sorrowful Son."

The gaze celebrated in the traditional Catholic iconography of the Son and Mother is made more dramatic by St. Alphonsus, who says the Son wiped from his eyes the clotted blood, which, as it was revealed to St. Bridget, prevented him from seeing, and looked at his Mother, and the Mother looked at her Son. Christ recognizes his own as his own recognize him.

He was, as Isaiah says, "One of those from whom men hide their faces," but his mother would not avert her eyes from him. Mary again is the model of compassion, teaching us to look in the face of suffering, despite the pain. Consolation means taking in some of the pain ourselves, but there is no option for those who truly love.

Jesus spoke to the crying women of Jerusalem and consoled them. The one who was suffering had compassion — if only we knew how to understand that insight, the world would be a different place. But Jesus says no such words to his mother. A look was enough to say, "We are in this together."

The solidarity of Mary was there for Jesus until the heart-wrenching parting. The thought of her following Jesus to Calvary must move us to deeper feelings of compassion. For Jesus, for Mary, for all the suffering.

We, too, have to give Jesus a shoulder and help him carry the cross. Union with Christ, that is the goal of our lives, as it was the blessing of Mary's. We need to pray for that communion in life that we receive sacramentally.

Mary, help us to be like you. Pray for us that we might wait with you for your Son on his way to Calvary. Look into the suffering of his face. Console him with our love. And follow him to the end. May the Lord grant that we keep company with you. Amen.

THE FIFTH SORROW

The Death of Jesus

In November, 1989, the guerrillas in El Salvador mounted the second of their so-called "final" offensives. Rumors had circulated for months about an attack on the main cities, a drastic change of venue for the fighting which usually consisted of skirmishes and army campaigns in the rural territory controlled by the revolutionaries.

We had a hint of the fighting to come when a group of Americans on one of the seemingly endless stream of "fact-finding" delegations that visited El Salvador were suddenly told to leave. A member of our mission team happened to know one of the visitors, and so we knew the day before that "something" was supposed to happen.

What happened was hellish. The guerrillas attacked San Salvador, surprised the army, and effectively took some neighborhoods hostage. Apparently, the guerrillas had the impression that the populace would rise up in arms. It did not. The other presumption, that the Salvadoran military would not bomb the houses of the people who lived in the capital city, also proved to be tragically incorrect.

The military, vengeful because of its own incapacity, struck out at the Jesuit professors at the Catholic University, who were vocal critics of government injustice. They killed six of the priests and two women who worked in the kitchen.

The city suffered terribly. The people, who, like everybody in the global village, see terrible situations in faraway places nearly every day on television, compared their situation to Beirut. Words cannot do justice to the whole drama of a modern city that becomes a field of battle. Violence where there had been domesticity, destruction where there had been construction, domiciles and churches converted into battle stations — the "final offensive" was an apocalyptic world upside down.

Our town was untouched by the fighting. There were rumors of an attack on the town which never materialized, although I spent a nervous night when the mayor stopped me on the street to tell me that it was our time. The dusk-to-dawn curfew was inconvenient, but it was nothing compared to suffering we heard of from San Salvador, where bodies were left for days in the streets, like something out of the Old Testament. My real worry was that our bishop from the United States would make good a threat to withdraw us from the country, something which I think would have devastated our parish.

I had no idea during the days of the offensive, during which we heard of the brutal sacrifice of the Jesuits, that there was a drama closer to us, one that involved a family well-known to us of the parish.

Dolores was a *desplazada*, someone who had fled the area of combat with what she and her family could carry and settled in a house on the edge of the dirty river that curved around an edge of our town. Poor and troubled, the family received some help from the church, and some members were very faithful in coming to Mass and prayers. Dolores had several children, of whom one, Antonio, had made confirmation the year before the offensive. That means that he was almost sixteen when he died.

How could we have thought at confirmation that the monster war would be consuming one of the fifteen-year-olds in the space of little more than a year? It makes me think of the old poem:

> Oh little did my mother know,
> the day she cradled me,
> The lands I was to travel in,
> the death I was to die.

All during the drama of the offensive, Dolores had had her own tragedy that she kept quiet about. Antonio, like more than a few others, had been recruited by the guerrillas to fight alongside the mercenaries and the veterans in the streets of the city. A friend of mine in the city had his parish commandeered by the guerrillas and witnessed the training given to the new recruits, mere boys, for a few days. They were then sent into the jaws of an army whose weaponry and training was financed by the greatest military power that has existed in the history of the world.

All the while people were talking about the horrible goings-on in San Salvador, Dolores waited for news. Even as I talked with officials of our San Salvador Diocese to allay the fears of our stateside superiors, the boy's mother heard nothing. As people went to the Masses we said for the Jesuits and complained about the curfew and the fact that leaving town was forbidden, Dolores was waiting to hear about her son. Most of us were fighting boredom; she was ready to explode from nerves.

She was telepathically at the foot of the cross, because from the start she had little hope. The dream of an urban insurrection had completely failed. Looking back on the fighting, one sees a crazed quality on both sides: the brutal army was matched by the hopelessly and cruelly naïve guerrilla movement. How could they have hoped what was so unlikely, how could they have involved so many more people in the awful risk of urban fighting?

Some weeks after the fighting, Dolores said her son was "missing." He had gone to visit relatives in San Salvador a few days before the fighting — that was the first story she told us. She feared that he was lost. Then, of course, that he had been killed. Finally, she told us that he had joined the guerrillas and had been armed for the so-called uprising. Clearly, she knew from the beginning what had happened, but had tried to include us in her sad denial.

The woman was obsessed by her son's death, which I think most natural. She had not been in a position to refuse her son permission, he was of an age in a macho culture when that is no longer an issue. Besides, no doubt she had lost family members to the savagery of the war. For many, the guerrillas were an inevitable choice for reasons of revenge, the old the-enemy-of-my-enemy-is-my-friend operative principle. The woman's problem was the seemingly infinite regret felt by parents at the death of their young, particularly when death seems to have been avoidable.

The basis of all these reflections has been a comparison between what happens in the present among the poor with the life and sorrows of the Blessed Virgin Mary. I take seriously the complexity of the present, where politics and conflict, injustice and violence, are inevitable aspects of life. They were also inevitable aspects of the life of Mary. The death of Jesus involved the political power structure; as we know from the example of Pontius Pilate, who, as the Spanish say, managed to get a mention for himself in the Apostles' Creed.

But, and we cannot hesitate a moment in adding, the death of Jesus had much more meaning than just an episode of unrest in a difficult time, a generation before the Jewish rebellion against Roman Empire, which ended in the destruction of the temple. It had a cosmic meaning beyond all time. This Son who died changed human history.

We cannot say that about this poor boy caught in the ideological tangle of our times. Unfortunately, his death made little difference in the world. But a mother's love knows more than history. Wordsworth told this story in his poem about a young love:

> She lived unknown, and few could know
> When Lucy ceased to be;
> But she is in her grave, and oh,
> The difference to me.

Eventually, more people in town figured out the truth about Antonio. But only his mother felt the tremendous difference his absence made.

A young man dead, a mother emotionally crippled by sadness. The trouble is that in places like El Salvador, this story is multiplied any number of times. There is a reality about war that perhaps only the mothers of those fighting can know. In El Salvador, this included the mothers of daughters because they fought in the guerrilla war, too. How many sorrowful mothers in the little country, how much grief wending toward despair!

Do I compare all these mothers to the Virgin Mary, whose Son was completely innocent? I don't think that Our Lady would reject the comparison. She would say, I am confident, "I know your grief." Although most of the mothers of the soldiers and guerrilleros were not actually present when their children died, the shadow of the cross darkened wherever they were.

One reason we meditate on the Seven Sorrows is to be better aware of the great example of Mary. The other is to give us confidence to approach her for help, in the form of both counsel and consolation.

I have seen in my life that the most sympathetic people are those who have suffered greatly. We can count on some people to feel for us, to make the effort necessary to understand, to take upon themselves some of the weight we feel on our shoulders. Mary is such a person. Trust her with your life, your heart, your soul. Her arms will as easily fold around you as they did around Jesus when she held his body taken from the cross.

Much has been written about Mary at the foot of the cross. How do you express the pain of the mother who stood for the whole Church there at Golgotha? St. John Chrysostom said that whoever was present at Calvary might have seen "two altars on which two great sacrifices were consummated; the one in the body of Jesus, the other in the heart of Mary."

I saw this maternal sacrifice replayed in Dolores' case — although not in the nobility of giving freely back to God life that came from him nor in a sense of the redemption of the world, which many insist Mary could instinctively feel. Dolores could see no such meaning in what was the tragedy of her life. What I saw was the pain that had to be there for Mary, too, the pain that makes the sacrifice all the more inspiring.

The mothers of guerrillas and the mothers of soldiers could go to Mary for comfort. They could say to her, "It was not fair. He was so young. I wish I had died first." Perhaps it is saying too much, but I believe there would be resonance in the Immaculate Heart for all the suffering.

Mary's vocation was communal. There was a hint of that at Cana, where Mary shows us that she is the advocate of the poor (it was cheap wine, and yet they ran out of it). Then there is Mary at the foot of the cross, the head of a small community of disciples, those who were left when the crowd stopped cheering.

That scene should be imbedded in our Christian consciousness. Jesus looks down on his mother, who stands with the other two Marys and the beloved disciple in the nineteenth chapter of John's Gospel. Again aware of the treasures that still hide in familiar texts, let us read what it says:

> When Jesus saw his mother,
> and the disciple there whom he
> loved, he said to his mother,
> "Woman, behold your son."

Then he said to the disciple,
"Behold your mother." And from
that hour, the disciple took her
into his home" (John 19:26-27).

When we think of the shortness of the Gospels, details like what is said in these two verses have to capture our attention. Jesus expressed a thought for his mother even as his every breath was more costly because of the form of his execution. Who will deny a universal implication in this solicitude?

The mother and the disciple, the two bound to the Lord by deep human love, are told to be each other's consolation. It is the only human inheritance that Jesus' left. The clothes off his back were confiscated, but the love of these two people was a treasure which he could bequeath. The words are a poignant testament. "Mother, I have nothing to give you but the love of this disciple. Youngest and bravest of my followers, I give you what was my life's greatest consolation, the love of the most valiant of maternal hearts."

The scene is at once particular and universal. It tells us a human story of the love of a poor mother and a poor son, and it tells us something about each one of us. Put yourself at the foot of the cross for a moment. Take John's place just for a few minutes. Note the order of Jesus' few words.

First, he offers comfort to the disciple by offering the one who had comforted and consoled him his whole life long. "Woman, behold your son." That was saying, "Mother, now you are to console this one, you are to love this one as a son." If a friend was dying and suggested that his mother would console us, how could we be unmoved by the gesture? Again, Jesus the afflicted, was paying attention to the suffering of others.

Then, the disciple, who stands at the foot of the cross with the heartbreak that only the young and idealistic can feel in all its sharpness. "This woman who suffers, she is your mother." The immediate nature of his response is emphasized by the phrase, "from that hour."

Looking up at the cross, think of some words to tell Jesus about this involvement with him and his mother. In so much religious art, John's arm embraces the shoulders of Mary. Reach out to Mary in the same way. I believe that John could forget his grief, keen as it was, in the desire to alleviate the sorrow of Mary. Relationship to Mary means more freedom from self, more compassion.

The presence of St. John in this sorrow underlines the main point of the devotion — which is to accompany Mary. She is the guide; she is the teacher of patience and peace; she is the one who can teach us to look beyond our sufferings to Jesus.

The old hymn known by its Latin title, "Stabat Mater," says what this Sorrow should leave us with. One translation has these two verses:

> Could a man for all his boldness
> Watch unmoved in silent coldness
> Christ's own mother suffer so?
>
> No man truly open-hearted

Seeing Mary broken-hearted
But would comfort her in woe.

Are you an open-hearted person? Stand by Mary in the shadow of the cross.

Mary, could I put my arm around your shoulders? I don't know if I should look up at the cross or into your eyes. Seeing your communion in his suffering takes my breath away. Let me stand here next to you. Let me soak in the painful grace of this moment. Amen.

THE SIXTH SORROW

Jesus Is Pierced by a Lance and Taken Down From the Cross

I still remember how his father came to me at seven o'clock in the morning to tell me that he had died.

"There is someone dead on the road outside of town," he said. "We need some help."

"Who is it?" I asked.

"My son," he said, and then pain twisted up his face.

It was not the first time that the boy had troubled his father. There are some people whose road never seems easy. Certainly they are responsible for part of their troubles, but their restlessness is so innate, and appears sometimes to go against their own wishes, that one can only say, "There, but for the grace of God, go I."

Juan was unlike his brothers and sisters. They were not known for their drinking, nor for their frequenting places with terrible reputations. They did not have scrapes with the law, nor did their friends make up the wildest group in town.

His body was about a block from a bar which was more than a bar. He had been stabbed. Whoever had dragged his body across the street to the ditch perhaps hadn't thought of the trail of blood that led back to the place. In the harsh light of the tropical morning, the dried blood could be traced on the black asphalt.

I went to buy a casket and then came back to where the body was. Of course, a crowd had gathered. People in the United States would be glued to the television screen; the poor of our town could see the real thing up close. I was not permitted to take the body away until the *juez* had come. The Justice of the Peace was eating breakfast, and so the family had to wait more than an hour.

Because I went to the house with the casket, I was not there when the ambulance-like vehicle from the forensic service arrived on the scene and the Justice of the Peace signed the paper that gave permission for burial. All violent and unexpected death required the verification of the J.P., and unfortunately, his appearance was more or less routine in El Salvador.

At the wake, the mother was even more distracted than she was in the morning. There were people everywhere in the house and yard, and out onto the street in front. Especially, I remember seeing the friends of the boy in front of the house. They grew silent as I approached. I could feel that they were angry at what had happened to Juan, but I did not guess what some of them would do that night.

The next morning, I passed the burnt shell of the rancho which was going to be the restaurant attached to the bar where Juan had been killed. The thatched roof of the place had been a work in progress for months, a beautiful weaving made of palm branches.

The consequences of the arson never entered my mind. I was on my way to Mass at a country chapel. The place was some distance away, and I figured I could do the confessions and the Mass in two hours and be back for the funeral Mass at 1:00 p.m.

I was done before I had expected to be. As I sat down to quick lunch at noon, a man who worked in the market came into the rectory. He had bad news for me. The authorities had gone to Juan's house and taken the casket with the body for an autopsy. It would be necessary to go to the city twenty kilometers away to recover the body. The chase was on. I got to the morgue only to discover that the workers were taking a lunch break. My concern was not only about the people who would be attending the Mass, but also the condition of the unembalmed body, which had baked in the sun and would already be in the process of decomposition. Besides, I was upset by the strange order for an autopsy when the young man had died of knife wounds. What could an autopsy establish?

Juan's father and another relative were at the morgue. He was relieved to see me because he hoped that I might command more respect than he did. Talking with him confirmed my suspicions about the whole incident. It turned out that the person who had killed Juan was the son of the lady who ran the bar that was more than a bar. This explained the act of revenge by the young friends of Juan.

It also explained the bizarre order for the autopsy. The Justice of the Peace was a friend of the mother of the murderer. He had a business that distributed beer and soda, and the owner of the bar was a client of his. The autopsy was ordered as an act of revenge for burning down the rancho. Its purpose was to somehow upset the funeral. It was like arresting the corpse for what had happened. The afternoon was a torture. Not only would no one explain why the order had been given, but there was a problem about us taking the body back for burial. I couldn't call from the morgue, but luckily was close to a convent of Franciscan nuns who lent me their phone to call several people in my efforts to get the poor boy's body back for Christian burial. My calls included one to a lawyer in a human rights agency, whose call to the morgue would eventually help.

But not before I would actually hear the work of the autopsy. I was waiting for the workers to come back, assuming that the autopsy was finished. I was wrong, and was forced to sit on the other side of a flimsy wall and hear the saw that opened up the young man's chest. The noise has stayed in my memory as a disgusting affront to justice and sensitivity.

What it reminds me of now is the way Jesus' side was pierced with a lance. St. Alphonsus Liguori, in his meditation on that sorrow, has the Blessed Virgin saying, "Ah, my son is already dead; cease to outrage him; torment me no more, who am his poor Mother." Theology has commented greatly on the symbolism of the piercing with a lance. St. Thomas Aquinas said that the water and blood that flowed from Jesus' side represents the birth of the Church. Great mystics have talked about the open heart of Jesus and of hiding within Christ's body.

But first of all, the piercing with the lance was an injustice. I know very well the feeling accompanying St.

Alphonsus' words, *"cease to outrage him!"* As if it were not enough to cut down a young man in the prime of his life, now his dead body would be abused. As it was with Juan, so with Jesus.

St. Bernard said "The lance which opened his side passed through the soul of the Blessed Virgin, which could never leave her Son's heart." Jesus could no longer feel the thrust of the lance, any more than Juan could feel the indignity of the autopsy that was a punishment. But there were others to feel.

It was one last insult. This had to hurt Mary. Surely just the sight of his dead body on the cross was cruel enough without another reminder of her vulnerability and absolute powerlessness to protect him whom she loved so deeply.

Who has not felt the pain associated with seeing for the first time the dead body of someone loved in life? It is like a silent and invisible blow to the heart. How often we are overwhelmed at the moment of the first viewing. How it makes us realize the suffering hidden in all our tenderness. The pain of loss takes on the mask of this shadow so like something else we knew, a person whom we loved and who loved us. I think I will remember all my life the gesture of my grandmother's brother who at her funeral service touched her cold hand in good-bye. My grandmother was not "there" but her memory was.

This is what the Sixth Sorrow is about. Now Mary's pain really is entirely her own. Despite her holy company, she is alone as she had not been while her son lived. The great secret of his life and hers had to be heavier now that he was no longer with her. Surely that thrust of the lance must have seemed to represent so much more. How she must have felt it. The saddest moment of her life and the one who was the greatest source of consolation, the person who with only a glance could give strength, was no longer there.

And then Jesus was taken down from the cross and his lifeless body placed in her arms. How many years since those arms had not felt his weight, and now it was crushingly heavy. No wonder Michelangelo was so inspired by the last embrace. The sadness of it can make your heart stop beating

Juan's mother had not been present as her husband and I heard what was going on in the other room in the morgue. As it turned out, his brother and I took his naked body in our arms and lowered him from the autopsy table to the casket on the floor. Even now, I can recall the rubbery embrace of his body. Thank God that Juan's mother was at home. She is a sensitive woman, a person who has suffered in so many other ways, and it was a special grace that she did not witness the injustice of it all.

In the other chapters, a woman's suffering has helped us to see Mary's sorrows more concretely. And yet in this reflection, the mother was not present. In fact, her absence is the basis of comparison this time. Mary was not spared in the same way. That is the point. Some people to whom I have told this story have objected to what they say is its depressive quality. They call it graphic; what they mean is indelicate. No doubt the crucifixion was offensive in a similar way.

The death of Jesus, at which Mary was present, was a terrible act of injustice. The Sixth Sorrow reinforces that injustice by making us imagine it through the experience of Jesus' mother. It makes me want to take Mary in my arms and comfort her somehow, shield her somehow from what is so ugly.

I suffered as a witness to what was done to a friend's son. How much more Mary suffered, because her identification with her son was as total as a human being is capable of. Any mental picture of the scene has to include two quite different elements: the extreme tenderness of the Blessed Virgin's love for Christ and the brutal callousness of his executioners. How disturbing it is to reflect on the two combining in the moment of the piercing.

It is even more disturbing to think of how often this suffering of Mary is echoed in the hearts of mothers throughout the world. How many living icons of Mary's grief are seen in this world of violence and hatred? How can we be insensitive to it all until it comes knocking at our door?

This Sorrow of Mary is a window that lets us see the world with a new perspective. We need to join Mary in that awful moment when she saw the lance and felt as if it pierced her body too. We need to feel the dead weight of the Beloved on our knees to understand the experience. The Sorrows of Mary are a school of compassion.

Think about some terrible thing that has hurt you, and hold that feeling. Magnify it; imagine how it would be if you could feel at the same time the absolute necessity of what happened, even the tearing apart of your heart, and an unspeakable love that was so mixed up with the pain that it was impossible to distinguish the two.

Then try to see Christ on the cross through Mary's eyes. See the soldier come closer; know that it doesn't matter any more — he is dead — but feel it deeply anyway. Sense how the perfect love of Mary must have attached her to the one who was perfectly lovable. Let the lance reach your own heart.

See them climbing up to take his body down from the cross. Let your own heart sink down as they lower this shell, this shadow of flesh.

So often we are wrapped up in ourselves. We do not feel the pain of others because we make all of life a drama at which we are the center. Sometimes even the pains of those close to us can become like props to us, part of our story instead of reasons for transcending our pettiness. The Sorrows of Mary, by making us focus on her and through her on the sufferings of others, can help us so much.

St. Albert the Great wrote some words that impress me because they talk about the source of compassion: "That you weep one tear of love: that is more pleasing to God than that you weep tears of regret or self-pity, even if they would flow as abundantly as the waters of the Danube." Can we have the heart to feel the pain of others, to take on the pain of the world instead of the steady inventory we make of our small sufferings? Can we put others first? That is something to meditate upon in terms of this sorrow of our mother.

Lord, stretch my heart. Give me freedom from my own suffering, so that I can comfort others in their suffering. Let my heart, like yours, be pierced open, open for all. Let me learn from your mother to stand by you. Give me some of her strength, and that part of her love for you of which I am capable. Amen.

THE SEVENTH SORROW

The Burial of Jesus

Since I have been home from the missions, I have felt a deep sense of loss. Missionaries apparently get so used to and fond of other places that it is difficult to adjust when they call us home. There are programs and retreats about the issues of returning missionaries, but I guess you have to go through a grief period no matter what else happens. It's a separation from what has become familiar, what has become home.

My personal experience makes up for my lack of imagination, I suppose. Now I feel as never before for those who are far from their country and loved ones.

The first Mass I said in a new city was a Spanish liturgy. I have found that some of my homesickness dissipated when I celebrate in my second language. Spanish is an emotional language, very expressive of moods and emotions. Something about prayer in Spanish permits me more fervor than I usually can muster in English.

I was in a new city, where I knew only one other priest. Finding the church was a little difficult, but I arrived with plenty of time to spare. In the sacristy, a woman struck up a conversation with me.

We began talking about Bible study, because she was looking for some books or study-guides to send to her children in Colombia. She was worried about their faith; she hoped that they could be sustained by Catholicism as she was in all her trials. One theme led to another and then the woman showed me some pictures of her family which she had in her purse.

Two pictures were of her son who had died. It was still difficult for her to talk about. One picture had been taken by some friend of his at a beach he had visited on Colombia's Pacific shore. He was smiling sheepishly at the camera, never thinking that in a few years this photo and another of a brother and him would be all that his mother could show to friends of his life.

"They killed him." In Spanish that is more common as a construction than, "he was killed." Who the killers were, she did not know. Only that her son was gone.

She had not been able to go to the funeral. Her job was cleaning houses, so her pay was minimal. The life she led was austere in extreme; every dollar that went for her rented room, clothes, and her food was one she could not send to Colombia to her other children. The average American cannot understand the hard-earned dollars that go to Third World countries so that sons, nephews, and grandchildren can go to school, or get medical attention, or have decent housing. Most immigrants, documented or not, work very hard for what they get, and often have lives that are severely circumscribed — from house to work and back, with very little to vary their schedule. They live like so many of our European ancestors who sweated and saved so that we would he able to live in the middle-class mainstream.

She did not know when she would be able to return to Colombia even to visit. The money for the airline ticket could be so useful in other ways. With all their needs, they had to be patient. How could she go home with nothing? What would she bring for the poor people back home? The expense of the trip would also mean months in which she could send no help home.When her son was killed, his brothers and sisters had buried the boy and she had to stay in the North.

Some people seek the faraway, but I doubt that there are many who do not want to go back home for special occasions. I talked to a nun once who said that she was not allowed to go home for her father's funeral when she was stationed in Hawaii. The order would not pay for the airfare. She was elderly, but I could see that the pain was still in her heart. Now things had changed; it would not have been a question, but in that sad moment she had not been able to comfort her mother, nor receive the comfort of family and friends.

How many times in life do we find that the right person at the right time, even if he or she is a stranger, can relieve us just by listening to our grief? Minutes after meeting this Colombian woman, I knew the saddest story of her life — the death of her son in the crime-ridden streets of the city from which she came.

We were in the sacristy of a church in an industrial city in New England, and our conversation had transported us across space and time, two things that the human heart has always felt cause suffering between people who love. Distance and death, the separations that love can conquer but which cost it dearly.

The poor photo was a relic of her son whom she would not see even when she finally returned to their home. She had to imagine how home would never be the same. When we are not permitted assistance at burials, I think the heart tries to play tricks on us. We may know of a death, but it does not come home to us; we do not have the opportunity to let it sink into our consciousness.

It is hard enough when we are present. One of the saddest things my mother ever told me was that she never got over the feeling of trying to call her mother after my grandmother died. Without thinking she had said, "I'll call Ma," picked up the phone and was dialing before she caught herself.

Our faith tells us that the separation of death is not definitive, but that is not immediately evident to the heart. The poet Emily Dickinson wrote that parting was all we know of heaven and all we need of hell. All we know of the hope of heaven, all we need of the pain of hell.

This last Sorrow of Mary is about separation. Her life would never be the same until she was with her son again. St. Augustine, who well knew about a mother's love, said that "With Christ crucified, the Mother was also crucified." The quick burial of Jesus because of the approaching Sabbath, the inability even to wash his body and perfume it as was the custom, the absence of most of his closest followers — all these elements must have made Mary suffer.

It was no doubt the saddest moment in her life, the culmination of all her fears and griefs. St. Bernard imagines Mary saying, "Having lost my only Son, I have lost all." What were her emotions at the tomb? Nothing shows the faith of Mary better than her silence — thus she offered to God the whole of the passion, death, and burial of Jesus. One time in her life she had asked an angel how something could be. He had called her to faith, which she had expressed immediately. One time she had questioned her Son, "How could you do this to us?" but had understood the answer required faith in the ministry. She was once with some relatives who feared for Jesus' well-being and even his sanity. She had said nothing, but must have had forebodings even then of the terror of his death.

But she was silent. The silence of Mary was eloquent — that is a theme that has inspired writers to so many words. But what thoughts did she have at the tomb?

In my family there is another story of loss and grief. My mother's father died suddenly of a heart attack when my mother was only ten — the same age my little sister would be when my father died. My mother, reflecting in the time after the death of my father on what she remembered about my grandfather's death, recalled something of the grief of her mother. My grandmother had revealed to her children that the day of the funeral she had said to herself at the graveside, "Raymond, how could you do this to me?"

Talking at gravesides is something people do in the movies but it is also something most of us have wanted to do at some point. What would Mary have been moved to say to Jesus?

Could she have thought, "Why have you left me?" Would she have been able to say, "My son, when will I see you again?" We can all try to imagine what she might have thought; this is not to take license, but to feel that one with whom we have a relationship might have thought this way. Considering her lifelong faithfulness, I think she may have thought, "Rest in peace, my child, rest as you did when I cradled you."

Michelangelo's *pietà* is famous because the statue shows a young Mary holding Christ. The sculptor said that he portrayed Mary that way because from the moment of her acceptance of the will of God for her, the death of Christ had been implicit. Just as she would hold him on her knees as a child, she was bound to hold his corpse in one last cradling.

Artists can feel and express truths that theologians never dream about. Certainly that is true of the *pietà*. What depths of meaning are in that last embrace of mother and son. Michelangelo, with the youthful Mary holding Christ, emphasizes both the closeness of the two and inevitably focuses on the pain of the one who could still feel pain. But what a serene Mary it is. That is why I think of her saying to Christ. "Rest in peace, my child, rest as you did when I cradled you." She was at peace because his sufferings had ended.

I have noticed how young mothers sometimes have a special closeness to the children of their youth, a closeness that almost blends in elements of the love of siblings. The short distance in years between Christ and Mary must have had a part in their affection for each other. And, obviously, such things sharpen the sense of loss. But she was at peace, a peace that the world cannot understand.

Here was her baby. The poor Colombian woman had shown me his picture saying, "Here is *mi niño* — my child."

It didn't matter that he had been a young man when he was killed. He was still her child. She could see him in terms of the story of his life and hers.

Pope John Paul II, whose motto, "Totus Tuus," refers to his complete devotion to Mary, has an interesting set of reflections on the way of the cross. At the Tenth Station, Jesus Stripped of His Garments, the Pope imagines the reaction of Mary. This wounded, defenseless, suffering body was the same one she had bathed as a child. In every way, the maternity of Mary was part of her discipleship.

As a mother she grieved. For that reason countless mothers have turned to her in their grief. Through centuries, mothers have turned to the one who preceded them in grief. The one who lost her son who was all.

As I sit here writing, I try to imagine people who might interest themselves in these reflections. Who knows what sorrows might be yours? I have no way of comforting you except to reassure you with the comfort of faith. Look at the case of Mary: what could she tell you of the pain of separation?

Another few verses of poetry come to my mind. Alfred Lord Tennyson wrote them about the death of a friend. They are familiar, but are sometimes understood in terms of failed romance. They are not about failed relationships, but about the loss that is death, and how love is always more important than death.

> I hold it true, whate'er befall;
> I feel it, when I sorrow most;
> 'Tis better to have loved and lost
> Than never to have loved at all.

The last Sorrow of Mary must leave us with some sense of her tremendous valor. I can easily imagine her telling us that love conquers all, that it is always better to have loved. Her life of discipleship is proof of that. She will stand by us when we have doubts. We have been thinking about sad stories of present-day people to illustrate the timelessness and universality of the Sorrows of Mary. But we have to move beyond the sadness to the strength of faith.

The Sorrows of Mary are about a valiant woman who, despite her poverty, her probable lack of education, her uniqueness which implied a kind of solitude, her tragic life, a disappointment symbolized by the death of her Son, was able to arrive at the invincible spring of the Resurrection.

We have dwelt on the sadness of life in order to see that faith is always stronger. In the Song of Songs, there is a line that says, "Love is as strong as death." In the Christian dispensation, we know that Love is even stronger than death.

All of these women that we have been talking about had an inner strength. If not, they could not have kept going, whether in the streets of La Libertad or in the slums of Nairobi. They were among life's great survivors. That is why they reminded me of Mary.

She was to perfection both the suffering and the valor of these women. There is an old Latin saying about the weakness of comparing things: *omnia metaphora claudicat.* Quite simply it means that all comparisons limp. There is always a danger that comparisons obscure instead of reveal. I hope that the stories of these real people that I have told here can help us to understand Mary better. My own reflection on these Sorrows has helped me deepen my love for Our Mother. More than ever I am convinced of her significance for all of us.

In some of the reading I have done preparing these reflections, I came across stories about the value of the devotion of the Seven Sorrows of Mary. St. Alphonsus was accused of giving examples that have a fable-like air about them. He tells one of a religious who prayed meditating on the Sorrows of Mary frequently. At the end of his life, suffering agonizing doubts, he was favored with the experience of Mary's solicitude.

The man was at the border of despair because of thoughts of past sins and was regretting the little good he felt he had done in his life. Mary says to him, "My son, why are you so overcome with sorrow? You comforted me in my sorrows; now Jesus sends me to console you. Be comforted and come with me to heaven." Some friends are so special that we can feel that they are a grace of God for us. They are both a protection and a consolation. The friendship of Mary is a blessing that way. One way to grow in that friendship is to be with her in sorrow. Offer her your company now in prayer, and that will help you come to the company of her Son.

Catholic folklore has much to say about Mary and her gracious friendship to sinners, how she can rescue us for Christ. The stories are sometimes told in ways that don't speak to our modern ideas, but there is a deep truth beneath them. God puts certain people in our way to help us remember him. I can easily see how the Blessed Mother represents for some both the voice of conscience and the tenderness of mercy.

Whether in the form of a scapular, a rosary, an image, or a devotion, the presence of Mary in the life of anybody can serve in the last resort to be the reminder that brings us back home to the Lord.

You are a friend of Mary. With her you share the love of our Lord Jesus Christ. Preserve that friendship. Prove yourself a friend in both joys and sorrows and you will be grateful forever.

Mary, we have come to the end of the devotion but not the end of the story. We know that the resurrection of your Son validated all your suffering and demonstrated the reason for your hope. Now that we have walked with you, we can appreciate even more the meaning of your Son's victory over death. May we go with you from mourning to morning. Amen.

How You Can Pray

The Seven Sorrows

First, think of each Sorrow, picturing what it describes. Then think of a current example in your life in which you can see a parallel to the Sorrow or the need for a virtue especially evident therein. Think of some words of comfort for Mary.

Say a decade of the Rosary. There are special rosaries made with seven decades, but you can count the Our Father, the ten Hail Marys, and the Glory Be on any rosary.

At the end of meditating, talk to Mary sincerely. Ask her to pray for you, that you, too, be strong in faith, confident in hope, generous in love.

As a last thought, try to think of the coronation of Mary by Jesus in heaven, which has been the subject of so much art. The Sorrows of Mary gave way to the joys of heaven. Think of what Jesus said to Mary welcoming her to heaven, and then what he will say to you.

Our Sunday Visitor...
Your Source for Discovering the Riches of the Catholic Faith

Our Sunday Visitor has an extensive line of materials for young children, teens, and adults. Our books, Bibles, booklets, CD-ROMs, audios, and videos are available in bookstores worldwide.

To receive a FREE full-line catalog or for more information, call **Our Sunday Visitor** at **1-800-348-2440**. Or write, **Our Sunday Visitor** / 200 Noll Plaza / Huntington, IN 46750.

Please send me: __ A catalog
Please send me materials on:
   __ Apologetics and catechetics   __ Reference works
   __ Prayer books   __ Heritage and the saints
   __ The family   __ The parish

Name_____
Address_____Apt._____
City_____State___Zip_____
Telephone (   )_____

A73BBABP

Please send a friend: __ A catalog
Please send a friend materials on:
   __ Apologetics and catechetics   __ Reference works
   __ Prayer books   __ Heritage and the saints
   __ The family   __ The parish

Name_____
Address_____Apt._____
City_____State___Zip_____
Telephone (   )_____

A73BBABP

 **Our Sunday Visitor**
200 Noll Plaza
Huntington, IN 46750
1-800-348-2440
OSVSALES@AOL.COM

Your Source for Discovering the Riches of the Catholic Faith